やさ日
まんが
JAPAN
ガイド

Yasanichi Manga

Guide to Japan:

JAPAN

Easy Japanese and Fun Manga

やさしい日本語と楽しいまんがで
日本を知る

小川清美 著

Orrin Cummins 英語監修

IBC

編 集 協 力 ＝ 株式会社MATCHA，杉本麗

イラスト (p.75) ＝ ナツザメ（@NATU_ZAME）

装　　　　幀 ＝ 久保頼三郎

＊本書には、訪日外国人向けのWEBサイト「MATCHA」の「やさしい日本語まんが特集」に掲載されたまんがを、書籍化にあたって編集・再構成した内容が含まれています。WEBサイトに初出のまんがにはURLを掲載していますので、ぜひ検索してみてください。

＊ This book contains edited versions of the *Yasashii Nihongo Manga* series published by MATCHA, an informational website for foreigners visiting Japan. Links to the original manga on MATCHA's website have been provided in this book. Be sure to check them out!

＊参考として掲載しているWEBサイトのリンクURLは、2022年4月現在のものです。リンクが切れていたり、アドレスが変更されたりしてページが表示されない可能性があります。予めご了承ください。

＊ The website URLs provided as references are operational as of April 2022. However, some links may stop working if their corresponding pages are taken down or their addresses are changed.

まえがき

　「日本に 来て 日本の 習慣に びっくりした」、「日本語を 話してみたけど、日本人が あなたの 日本語が わからなかった」…… そんなことが ありませんか？

　わたしは、毎日 そんな 話を 生徒から 聞きます。その 話を まんがにして、MATCHAという 日本を 紹介する サイトに 毎月 のせてもらいました。そして、たくさんの 人の おかげで、これらの まんがを、この１冊の 本に することが できました。

　また、日本には 地震や 台風などの 災害が たくさん あるので、そのための 情報も、あたらしく まんがと 一緒に かきました。

　みなさんが この本を 読んで、日本の 旅行と 生活を 楽しめるといいな と思います。

小川 清美

Preface

You traveled to Japan, only to be surprised by the country's customs. You studied Japanese, but Japanese people don't understand you when you speak. Sound familiar?

I hear stories like this daily from my students. So, I created a manga series depicting those stories. I was then fortunate enough to have the stories published monthly on MATCHA, a website that provides information about Japan. And thanks to the assistance of many individuals, I have been able to publish all these manga in this book.

I also created some new manga to convey information about the many earthquakes, typhoons, and other natural disasters that occur in Japan.

My hope is that reading this book will help you enjoy your travel and daily life in Japan.

Kiyomi Ogawa

Contents

Column

「日本の価値ある文化が、時代とともに残っていく。」

　MATCHAは、そんな気持ちで株式会社MATCHAが作っている、日本に来る人のための観光メディアです。

　日本には、芸能（歌舞伎、能）、食べ物、工芸など、すばらしい文化があります。さらに最近は、アニメやまんがなどのポップカルチャーも生まれています。

　こうしたすばらしい日本文化と、それを知りたいと思っている外国の人たちをつなぐために、MATCHAは2013年12月に始まりました。MATCHAは、観光、おいしい食べ物、文化、便利な情報など、日本についての記事を10言語で書いています。そして今は、日本に来る人のための観光メディアの中で、一番大きなメディアの1つになりました。新型コロナウイルスが広がる前は、世界240以上の国と地域に、毎月340万ユーザーがいました。

　新型コロナウイルスのせいで観光客が外国から日本に来ることができなくなったので、MATCHAでは、日本の生活情報を集めた特集「Living in Japan」を作って、日本に住んでいる外国人が便利な情報を見ることができるようにしています。

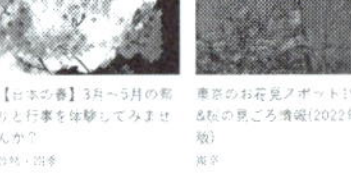

"Preserving Japan's valuable culture as time marches on."

Founded on this idea, MATCHA is a tourism media company dedicated to bringing people to Japan.

Japan is home to wonderful cultural aspects such as entertainment (*kabuki* and *noh*), food, and traditional crafts. And lately, pop-culture phenomena like manga and anime have also become quite popular.

MATCHA was established in December 2013 to help connect this incredible Japanese culture to foreigners who want to learn more about it. Our website contains articles about Japan written in 10 languages and featuring useful information about sightseeing, delicious cuisine, and other culture. MATCHA has become the largest tourism media company working to attract people to Japan. Prior to the coronavirus pandemic, as many as 3.4 million users from 240 countries around the world visited Japan every month.

The pandemic prevented tourists from visiting Japan from overseas, so MATCHA has switched gears to create its Living in Japan series, which includes information that is useful to foreigners living in Japan.

MATCHAの「やさしい日本語まんが特集」

MATCHA's Yasashii Nihongo Manga Series　　＊https://matcha-jp.com/easy/manga

　MATCHAには、普通の 日本語の 記事の 下に「やさしい日本語」の 記事を 見ること が できる ボタンが あります。世界 中 の 日本語を 勉 強 している 人が、日本の いい と ころを 知ることが できるように、作りました。

　記事は、日本語能 力 試験（JLPT）の 4級（N4）ぐらいの 文法と 単語を 使っていま す。そして、漢字には ふりがな、カタカナには 英語が 書いてあります。日本語を 学び 始めたばかりの 人でも、簡単に 読めるように しています。

　さらに、日本語が もっと 楽しく 学べるように、2019年に「やさしい日本語 まんが特 集 」を 始めました。「にこにこ にやにや」「さむい つめたい」のような、使いかたを ま ちがえやすい 日本語、また「納豆の 食べかた」など 外国人に わかりづらい 日本文化に ついて、まんがで わかりやすく 伝えています。ぜんぶで 40本以 上 を MATCHAの サ イトで 見ることが できます。

On the MATCHA website, there is button that allows users to view Yasashii Nihongo, which are easier versions of the regular Japanese-language articles. This was created so that people all over the world who are studying Japanese can learn about the amazing things the country has to offer.

The articles are written using vocabulary and grammar that is roughly equivalent to the N4 level of the Japanese Language Proficiency Test (JLPT). The kanji also has furigana above it, and English translations are provided for the katakana words. This makes the articles easy to read, even for people who have just started learning Japanese.

To make learning the Japanese language even more fun, we launched our Yasashii Nihongo Manga Series in 2019. This collection of comics provides simple explanations of tricky-to-use Japanese word pairs (like *nikoniko/niyaniya* or *samui/tsumetai*) as well as some facets of Japanese culture that foreigners sometimes struggle with, such as how to eat *natto*. Over 40 of these manga articles are available to view on the MATCHA website.

クリスティーヌ Christine

日本（にほん）の伝統文化（でんとうぶんか）が好（す）き。

Christine likes traditional Japanese culture.

林（りん） Rin

日本語（にほんご）の学校（がっこう）の学生（がくせい）。話（はな）すこととカタカナを練習（れんしゅう）している。

Rin is a student at a Japanese language school. He is studying speaking and katakana.

ラジープ Rajeep

日本（にほん）の会社（かいしゃ）で働（はたら）いているエンジニア。まじめ。

Rajeep works for a Japanese company as an engineer. He has a serious personality.

スリ Suri

日本語（にほんご）の学校（がっこう）の学生（がくせい）。少年（しょうねん）マンガが好（す）き。

Suri is a Japanese-language student who likes *shounen manga* (Japanese comics for boys).

高橋（たかはし） Takahashi

ラジープの会社（かいしゃ）の親切（しんせつ）な先輩（せんぱい）。

Takahashi is a kind-hearted senior employee of the company where Rajeep works.

山田（やまだ） Yamada

生（い）け花（ばな）教室（きょうしつ）の先生（せんせい）。クリスティーヌに伝統（でんとう）文化（ぶんか）を教（おし）えている。

Yamada is the instructor of an *ikebana* (flower arrangement) class. She teaches Christine about traditional Japanese culture.

小川（おがわ） Ogawa

日本語（にほんご）の学校（がっこう）の先生（せんせい）。林（りん）とスリに日本語（にほんご）を教（おし）えている。

Ogawa is a teacher at a Japanese-language school. She teaches Japanese to Rin and Suri.

Part
1
まちがえやすい日本語
Tricky Japanese Expressions

「はい」「いいえ」
Yes. / No.

*https://matcha-jp.com/easy/8530

スーパーや コンビニなどで、店の人は、袋が ほしいか どうか 聞きます。
中国人学生の 林は、袋が ほしい と思いましたが、店の人は 林は 袋が ほしくない と思って しまいました。

At supermarkets and convenience stores, cashiers ask if you need a plastic bag. Rin, a Chinese student, wanted a bag, but the cashier misunderstood his response.

"Hello."

"That will be ¥108. You don't need a plastic bag, right?"
"Oh…*hai.*"

"Okay, then I'll just put a sticker on it."　"Huh?"

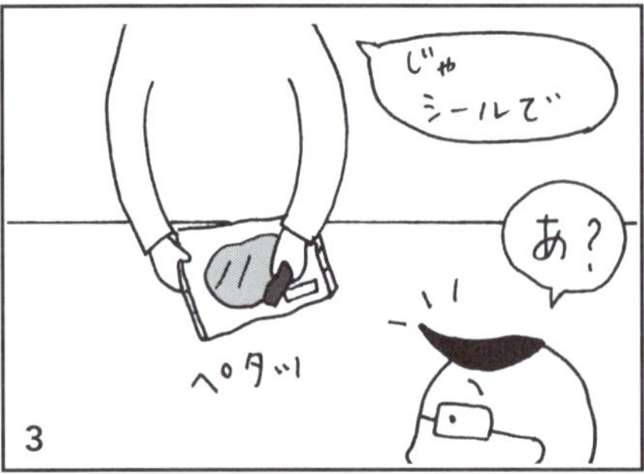

"What…?"　"A bag, please!"

否定形の答えかた
How to answer negative questions

店の人は「袋、いりませんか」と 否定形の 質問を しました。
日本人は「はい、いりません」と 否定形の 答えでも「はい」と答えます。
The cashier asked a negative question: "You don't need a plastic bag?"
Japanese people respond *hai* (*irimasen*) even when the answer is negative.

英語と 比べてみましょう。
Let's compare Japanese and English.

「袋、いりませんか？」　　You don't need a plastic bag?

「はい、いりません」　　No, I don't.

「いいえ、いります」　　Yes, I do.

英語の「right」と 同じで、日本人は「はい」と 言います。
The Japanese reply *hai* is equivalent to responding "right" in English.

でも、袋が ほしいときは、「袋ください」、「袋おねがいします」、「袋に 入れてください」など、はっきりと 言ったほうが いいです。
When you need a plastic bag, you should state that clearly. "Can you give me a plastic bag?" "A bag, please." "Can you put it in a bag?"

袋が ほしくないときは、「袋いりません」または「いらないです」と 言います。
And if you don't need one, you can say "I don't need a bag" or "I don't need one."

"Excuse me, could you put it in a plastic bag?"
"Sure."

いろいろな返事の仕方　Various Ways to Respond

YES / NO

日本語には、「はい」と「いいえ」だけでなく、いろいろな 返事の 仕方が ありま
す。また、「はいはい」「そうそうそう」「いえいえ」「いやいや」と、よく リピート
します。

There are ways to say "yes" and "no" in Japanese other than *hai* and *iie*. Some of the
commonly used responses contain repetitive syllables, such as *haihai*, *sousousou*, *ieie*, and
iyaiya.

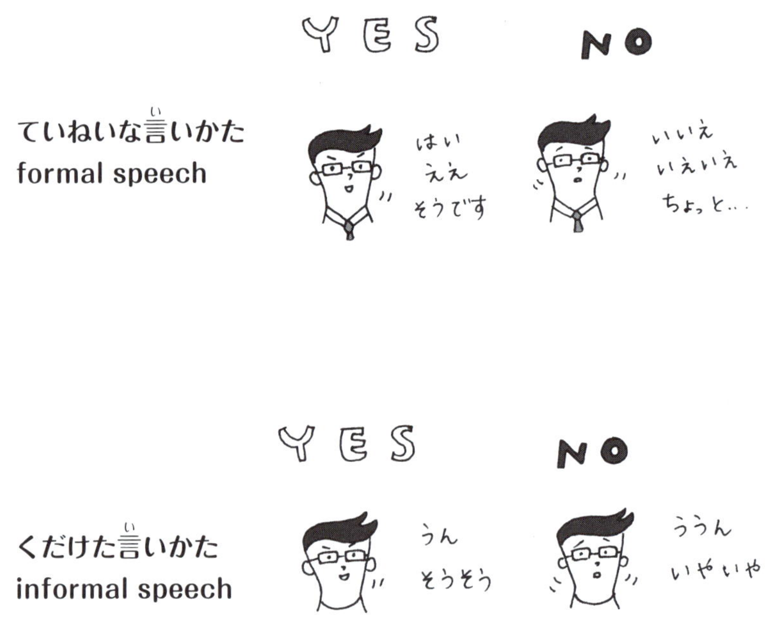

1 日本人は「いいえ」の 代わりに「すみません、ちょっと……」を よく 使います。この「ちょっと」は「ちょっとむずかしい」という 意味です。

Japanese often say *sumimasen, chotto...* instead of *iie*. This *chotto* is short for *chotto muzukashii* ("that's a little difficult").

2 感謝するときに、ときどき「すみません」と 言います。英語の I feel bad. と にています。

When people are grateful, they sometimes say *sumimasen*. This is similar to saying "I feel bad (for receiving this)" in English.

袋　Bags
（ふくろ）

2020年から レジ袋の ルールが 変わりました。全部の 店で レジ袋を もらうには お金を はらわないといけません。1枚1円から 5円くらい です。

The law regarding plastic bags changed in 2020. Now, you have to pay to receive bags at cash registers throughout Japan. They cost ¥1 to ¥5 each.

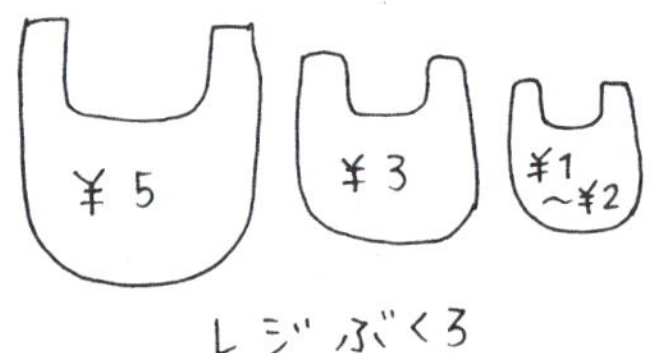

自分の 買い物袋（マイバッグ または エコバッグ とも 言います）を 持って 行ったほうが いいでしょう。

You should bring your own bag when you go shopping: *mai baggu* ("my bag") or *eco baggu* ("eco bag").

＊「かばん」も bag ですが、買い物には 使いません。
A *kaban* is also a bag, but it isn't used for shopping.

贈り物 Gifts

贈り物は、「つつんでください」と 言います。「プレゼントです」だけ でも だいじょうぶです。

When you need gift wrapping, say *tsutsunde kudasai*. You can also just say *purezento desu*.

ラッピングサービスは、たいてい無料ですが、有料の場合もあります。

Gift wrapping is usually free, although sometimes you will need to pay.

ときどき、箱に「のし」という 紙を つけます。「のし」に 何のための 贈り物か 書いてあります。

Some gifts are wrapped with a paper called *noshi* (sometimes a strip is placed on top). You can tell what occasions these gifts are for when you see them.

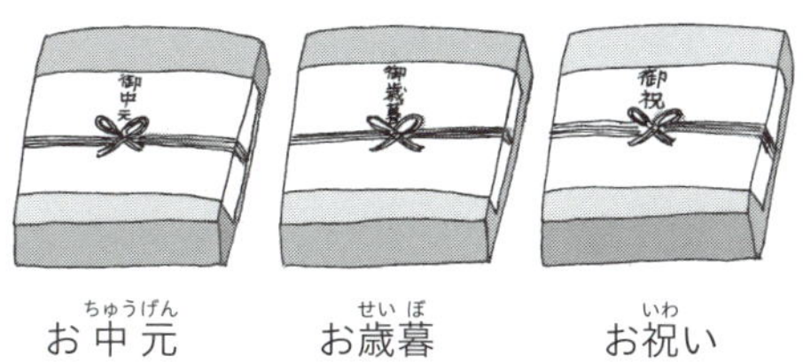

お中元　　お歳暮　　お祝い

ochugen (mid-year gifts), *oseibo* (year-end gifts), *oiwai* (celebration).

助詞
Particles

日本語には、たくさんの 助詞が あります。「は」「が」「へ」「に」「で」「と」「を」などです。
助詞を まちがえると、意味が 変わってしまいます。
日本語の クラスで、先生が 動詞を 教えています。どの 助詞を 使えば いいでしょうか。

Japanese has many particles such as は、が、へ、に、で、と、and を.
If you use the wrong particles, the meaning of the sentence will change.
A teacher is teaching verbs in a Japanese class. Which particle is used for each verb?

"What did you do yesterday?"

"I went **at** the supermarket."   "**To** the supermarket!!"

"What did you buy at the supermarket?"

"Well…Banana bought the supermarket!"
(Banana) "I bought the supermarket!"
"The particles are wrong…"

まちがえやすい助詞

Tricky particles

［場所：place］へ【e】/ に

家に（へ）　行く、来る、帰る　など。
英語の to と同じですが、住む、ある、いる　も「に」を 使います。このとき、「へ」
は使いません。

to [place]

go, come, return, etc.

This is similar to the English "to." However, you can also use に for "to live" and "there is/are." In these cases, へ cannot be used.

［場所］で

家で　食べる、会う、仕事する　など。
英語の at と in と同じです。「買う」も 使います。

at/in [place]

eat, meet, work, etc.

This is similar to the English "at" or "in." It can also be used for "buy from."

"I went **to** the supermarket yesterday.
I bought bananas **at** the supermarket."

「に」と「で」の他<ruby>他<rt>ほか</rt></ruby>の使<ruby>使<rt>つか</rt></ruby>いかた　Other usages of に and で

時間<ruby>時間<rt>じ かん</rt></ruby>と日<ruby>日<rt>ひ</rt></ruby>にち　Times and Dates

毎日<ruby>毎日<rt>まいにち</rt></ruby>、朝<ruby>朝<rt>あさ</rt></ruby>6時<ruby>時<rt>じ</rt></ruby>に 起<ruby>起<rt>お</rt></ruby>きます。
I wake up at 6 every morning.

3時半<ruby>時半<rt>じ はん</rt></ruby>に スーパーに 行<ruby>行<rt>い</rt></ruby>きます。
I went to the supermarket at 3:30.

{朝<ruby>朝<rt>あさ</rt></ruby>、昼<ruby>昼<rt>ひる</rt></ruby>、夜<ruby>夜<rt>よる</rt></ruby>、今日<ruby>今日<rt>きょう</rt></ruby>、明日<ruby>明日<rt>あ す</rt></ruby>、昨日<ruby>昨日<rt>きのう</rt></ruby>}の 後<ruby>後<rt>あと</rt></ruby>は、「に」を つけません。
Don't put に after morning, noon, evening, today, tomorrow, or yesterday.

× 　3月<ruby>月<rt>がつ</rt></ruby>に15日<ruby>日<rt>にち</rt></ruby>に火曜日<ruby>火曜日<rt>か よう び</rt></ruby>に3時半<ruby>時半<rt>じ はん</rt></ruby>に
○ 　3月<ruby>月<rt>がつ</rt></ruby>15日<ruby>日<rt>にち</rt></ruby>火曜日<ruby>火曜日<rt>か よう び</rt></ruby>の3時半<ruby>時半<rt>じ はん</rt></ruby>に

時間<ruby>時間<rt>じ かん</rt></ruby>と 日<ruby>日<rt>ひ</rt></ruby>にちを たくさん 言<ruby>言<rt>い</rt></ruby>うときは、最後<ruby>最後<rt>さい ご</rt></ruby>に 1回<ruby>回<rt>かい</rt></ruby>だけ 「に」を つけます。
When you say multiple time and date words together, you only put one に at the end.

いろいろな 使(つか)いかたが あります。 *De* has various usages.

方法(ほうほう)　with / by

なにで？
With what?

with chopsticks　　with a fork and knife　　with your hands

go by bike　　　　　watch on TV

〜でいい　fine with / OK with

Drinks?
Will that be all?　　　　Water is fine.
　　　　　　　　　　　Yes, that's it.

ひと + で　Number of people + *de*

一人(ひとり)で 行(い)きます。
I'll go by myself.

家族(かぞく)で 行(い)きます。
I'll go with my family.

いろいろな助詞　Various Particles

は・が

主語の 後に つけます。英語には ありません。

These are placed after the subject of the sentence. English doesn't mark the subject like this.

「は」は、普通の 文に 使います。
「が」は、疑問文と 主語を 強く 言うときに 使います。

Wa is used for regular statements.
Ga is used for asking questions or emphasizing the subject.

I am Suri.

Who?

Me!

〜はどう？　は、いつも「は」を 使います。

Always use *wa* for "How about…?"

Which one do you recommend?
How about this?

特別な使いかた　Special usage of *wa* and *ga*

{すき、きらい、じょうず、とくい、へた、にがて}の文は、いつも「SはOが…」です。

For sentences that describe likes (*suki*), dislikes (*kirai*), or being good (*jōzu* / *tokui*) or bad (*heta* / *nigate*) at something, always use the sentence structure [<Subject> *wa* <Object> *ga*…].

Christine **likes** Japan.

Rajeep is **good at** Japanese.

を

目的語の 後に つけます。発音は、ときどき wo ですが、たいていは o です。英語には ありません。

This is placed after the object of the sentence. The pronunciation is usually *o*, but sometimes people pronounce it *wo*. English doesn't mark sentence objects like this.

Suri watched anime.

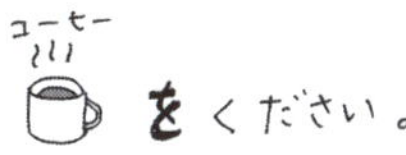

Please bring me some coffee.

と

単語と 単語を つなげます。
英語の and です。

This particle is used to connect words. It is "and" in English.

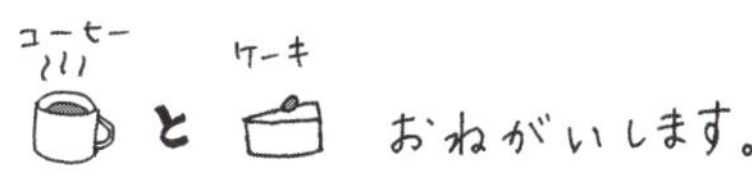

Coffee and cake, please.

with someone の 使いかたも あります。

It also used as "with someone."

Rajeep will eat a meal with Takahashi.

＊「は」「が」「を」は、省略できます。 You can leave *wa, ga, o* out.

　　　高橋さん　ごはん　食べました。 Takahashi ate a meal.

しかし、「（ひと）と ごはんを 食べる」と 言いたいときは、「と」は 言わなければ いけません。

But if you want to say that you ate a meal *with* someone, you have to use と after their name.

　　　高橋さん　と　ごはん　食べました。 I ate a meal with Takahashi.

「〜を出る」「〜が出る」

o deru versus *ga deru*

＊https://matcha-jp.com/easy/8163

ラジープは 日本の 会社で 働いています。
今日は 会議が あるようです。 しかし、ラジープは かんちがいを してしまいました。

Rajeep is working for a Japanese company.
It seems he has a meeting today. However, he has misunderstood something.

"Rajeep, the meeting at three *dete*."
"OK"

2:58 Almost time…

"Alright, I exited."
"What?!!" "Huh!!"

"Head into the meeting room."
"Why do I have to enter again? "
"Are you asking why…?"

「出る」の意味
The meaning of *deru*

「出る」は いろいろな 意味が あります。助詞が 違います。

The word *deru* has various meanings, each of which uses a different particle.

~に出る to attend or participate; to appear

大会に 出る participate in a competition

映画に 出る appear in a movie

~を・~から出る to leave

家を 出る   leave the house

映画館から 出る   exit the movie theater

~が出る to flow out of; to come out

鼻水が 出る have a runny nose

咳が 出る have a cough

助詞が ないときは、「出る」の 前のことばに 気をつけましょう。

If you don't see a particle in the sentence, pay attention to the words before *deru*.

《例 Ex.》 会議、出る attend the meeting 会議室、出る exit the meeting room

"I said *kaigi ni deru*."

"I thought *kaigishitsu o deru*."

"Hahaha"

出席・欠席について　Attendance and absence

「出席」は「出る」と 同じ 意味で、ていねいな ことばです。会議や 式、学校など で使われます。休むときには「欠席」という ことばを 使います。

Shusseki is a more formal way to say *deru*. It is used when referring to attending meetings, ceremonies, school, etc. For absences related to such events, *kesseki* is used.

学校で　At school

Is Rin here?

He's absent.

会社で　At the office

仕事には「出勤」「欠勤」を 使います。

For work, use *shukkin* (attend) or *kekkin* (don't attend).

朝8時に 出勤します。

I arrive at work at 8 in the morning.

今日 休みます。欠勤届けは 後で 出します。

I'm taking the day off. I'll submit my *kekkin todoke* (report of absence) later.

ツアーで　On a tour

旅行や ツアーには「参加」「不参加」を 使います。

For tours, use *sanka* (participate) or *fusanka* (don't participate).

ツアーに 参加します。

We participated in a tour.

結婚式に出席する　Attending a wedding

たいてい 郵送で 招待状 が 来ます。返信の ための ハガキも、封筒の 中に 入っています。

Usually, you will receive an invitation in the mail. The postcard used to R.S.V.P. is included with the invitation.

東京都〇〇
山田花子様 行

返信の ための ハガキには、相手の 住所と 名前が 書いてあります。名前の 下に「行」という 漢字が 書いてあるので、これを 二重線で 消して、「様」を 書きます。

The enclosed postcard for responding will list the other party's name and address. There will be a 行 under the name. Cross that out and write 様 (Mr. or Ms.).

＊会社や 団体の 場合は「御中」と 書きます。

If it's a company or organization name, write 御中 (Messrs.).

御芳名クリスティーヌ・スミス
御住所 東京都〇〇
（どちらか〇で囲みください）
御欠席
御出席 させていただきます。

出席の 場合、「御出席」に 〇を つけて、「御欠席」は 二重線で 消します。他の「御」も 全部 二重線で 消します。「御」は、招待客 への 尊敬を あらわしているからです。

If you will be attending, circle 出席 and cross out 御欠席. Also, cross out all the 御 as a sign of respect.

「させて いただきます」を ひらがなで 書きます。

Write *sasete itadakimasu* ("I will be honored to") in hiragana.

結婚式　Weddings

日本には、神道式の 結婚式が ありますが、今は 西洋式が 人気です。

Traditional Japanese weddings are in the shinto style. But lately, Western-style weddings are very popular.

神道式は 神社

Shinto weddings are held in a shrine.

西洋式は 教会や ホテル

Western weddings are held in a church or a hotel.

神道式と 西洋式の どちらも、ゲストは 白い服を 着ては いけません。白は 花婿と 花嫁の 色だからです。また、派手な 色や デザインも よく ありません。

You can't wear white clothes to either style of wedding, since that color is for the bride and groom. Flashy colors or designs are also inappropriate.

男の人は 黒か ダークカラーの スーツを 着ます。ネクタイは 黒ではなく 明るい 色が いいです。女の人は 黒や 紺、パステルカラーが いいです。

Men should wear black or dark-colored suits, but with a colorful tie rather than a black one. For women, black, navy, or pastel colors are appropriate.

お金を 祝儀袋 という 封筒に 入れて、受付で渡します。

Put some money in a special envelope called *shuugibukuro* and hand it in at the reception.

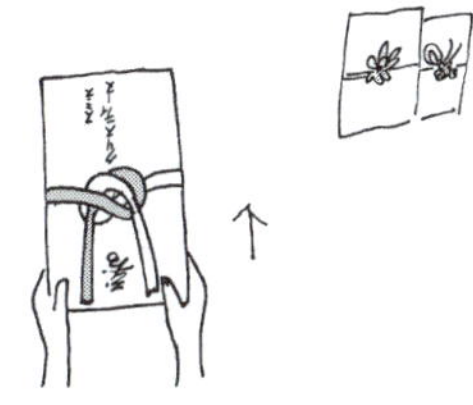

いろいろな 祝儀袋 があります。スーパー、コンビニ、インターネットなど、どこでも 買うことが できます。

There are various designs for *shuugibukuro*. You can find them everywhere: supermarkets, convenience stores, Internet shopping sites, etc.

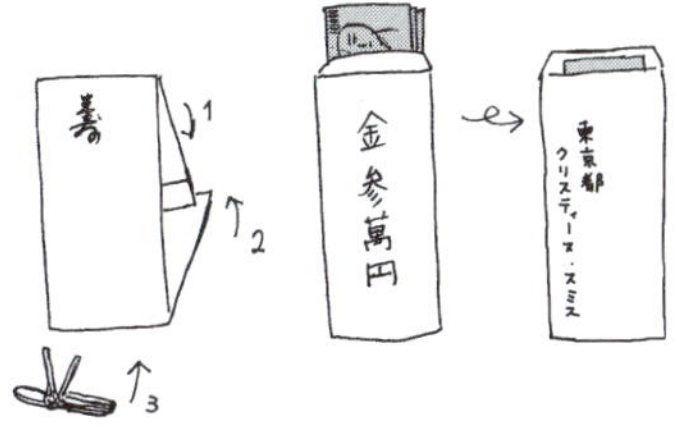

新しい お札を 入れます。
銀行や ホテルで 交換してもらうことが できます。

Use new, unwrinkled bills. You can exchange some old bills at a bank or hotel.

金額は1, 3, 5など 奇数（2で 割ることが できない 数）を 選びます。2人が 別れない という 意味です。封筒に 金額を 書きます。たいてい 古くて 難しい漢字を 使いますが、ふつうの漢字でも だいじょうぶです。

10,000 yen　→　壱萬円 (古い 漢字)　　　一万円 (ふつうの 漢字)

When deciding how much money to give, choose a number that is not divisible by two (an odd number). This signifies that the newlyweds will never separate. Write the total amount on the envelope (usually, writing it in the old-style format of kanji is required, but normal kanji are also acceptable).

「ときどき」「どきどき」

tokidoki versus *dokidoki*

＊https://matcha-jp.com/easy/7925

先生が 日本語 教 室で、みんなに「何を しますか」と 聞きました。
林と スリは 楽しそうに 話していますが、二人は ちがうことを 考えていま
す。

In a Japanese class, the teacher asks everyone, "What do you do?"
Rin and Suri are having fun talking about that topic. But, it seems they are
thinking about two different things.

"What do you do, everyone?"

"I study everyday.
Also swimming…but only sometimes."   "Oh! Me too!"

"You too?"

"Swimming is *dokidoki* (risqué)!"

"Ms. Suri, you should say *tokidoki* (sometimes)."

"Let's do it together!"
"I'm nervous."

「ときどき」と「どきどき」
tokidoki and *dokidoki*

気づきましたか？　林は「ときどき」と 言いましたが、スリは「どきどき」だ と 思いました。

Did you notice? Rin said *tokidoki* but Suri thought he meant *dokidoki*.

ときどき　*tokidoki*

英語の sometimes です。漢字の「時」が 語源です。

Tokidoki means "sometimes" in English. The word is derived from the kanji for time (時).

《例 Ex.》　ときどき、おすしを 食べます。

I sometimes eat sushi.

どきどき　*dokidoki*

英語の excited もしくは nervous です。心臓の 音が 語源です。

Dokidoki means "excited" or "nervous" in English. The word comes from the sound of a heartbeat.

《例 Ex.》　スピーチを したとき、どきどきしました。

When I gave the speech, I was nervous.

"I watch anime every day.
I sometimes read Japanese comics, too."

濁音　Dakuon

まんがで 見たように、「と」が 「ど」に なると、意味が 変わりましたね。この「゛」（てんてん）が ついた音は、「濁音」と 言います。

As we saw in the manga, changing と to ど can also change the meaning of the word. These two dots are called *dakuon* or simply *ten-ten*.

「くすくす」と「ぐずぐず」

くすくす：小さい 声で 笑っている　*kusukusu* : giggling

スリが くすくす 笑ってる。
Suri is giggling.

ぐずぐず：なにかを するのが 遅い　*guzuguzu* : doing something slowly (negative nuance)

林が ぐずぐずして 先生は 怒りました。
The teacher is upset at Rin's slow progress.

「ぱらぱら」と「ばらばら」

ぱらぱら：少ない 様子　*parapara* : just a little <action or state>

雨が、ぱらぱら 降っている。
The rain is falling a little.

ばらばら：散らかっている 様子　*barabara* : the state of being scattered

本が、ばらばらに なっている。
The books are scattered.

濁音は、強い 音も 表します。
Dakuon can also express the strength of a sound.

とんとん：軽く たたく　*tonton* : hit gently or lightly
どんどん：強く たたく　*dondon* : hit strongly

オノマトペ　Onomatopoeia

「どきどき」や「ぱらぱら」などの ことばを「オノマトペ」と 言います。音や 食感、気持ちなどを 表すときに よく 使います。

Phrases like *dokidoki* and *parapara* are collectively known as "onomatopoeia." These expressions are used to express a wide variety of sounds, textures, and emotions.

日本人は オノマトペが 大好きです。大人も 子どもも、男性も 女性も よく 使います。

Japanese people love onomatopoeia! Men, women, and children of all ages use them often.

Let's wipe that. It's a doggy!　　　smooth hair　prickly beard　　　Hurry up!

学校で オノマトペの テストも あります。

At school, students even have to take onomatopoeia tests.

ムスリムの生活と観光情報
Living and tourism information for Muslims

スリは ムスリムです。ムスリムの 人が 日本で 観光や 生活を すると
き、いろいろな 問題が あるかもしれません。しかし、学校や 市役所、
観光案内所で 相談すれば、だいじょうぶです。

Suri is a member of the Islamic faith. Muslims who live or sightsee in Japan
might sometimes encounter problems. These can be avoided, however, by
asking questions at your school, city office, or tourism office.

"I'm Muslim, so when I see bathing
suits, it makes me nervous."

"Hot spas, bathing suits, pork, and
alcohol are not allowed."

"A private spa, burkini, and your own
lunch box are OK!"

食べ物 Food

ハラルフードが 買える 店が あります。「業務スーパー」という 大きな
スーパーは、日本の いろいろな ところにあります。

Some shops have halal food. Gyomu Super, a large
supermarket, is one such store with many locations
throughout Japan.

* https://www.gyomusuper.jp/english/

東京には、たくさん ハラルレストランも あります。

Tokyo has quite a few halal restaurants.

* http://minato-intl-assn.gr.jp/halal_shop

礼拝（れいはい） Salah

旅行（りょこう）の ときに 礼拝（れいはい）を するのは 難（むずか）しいですが、空港（くうこう）、大（おお）きな 駅（えき）、有名（ゆうめい）な 観光地（かんこうち）や ショッピングモールに 礼拝所（れいはいじょ）が あります。

While it can be difficult to perform Salah while traveling, you can find prayer spaces in airports, larger train stations, shopping malls, and famous tourist spots.

モスク（マスジッド）も あります。

There are mosques (masjid) in Japan.

主要（しゅよう）なモスク　Main Mosques

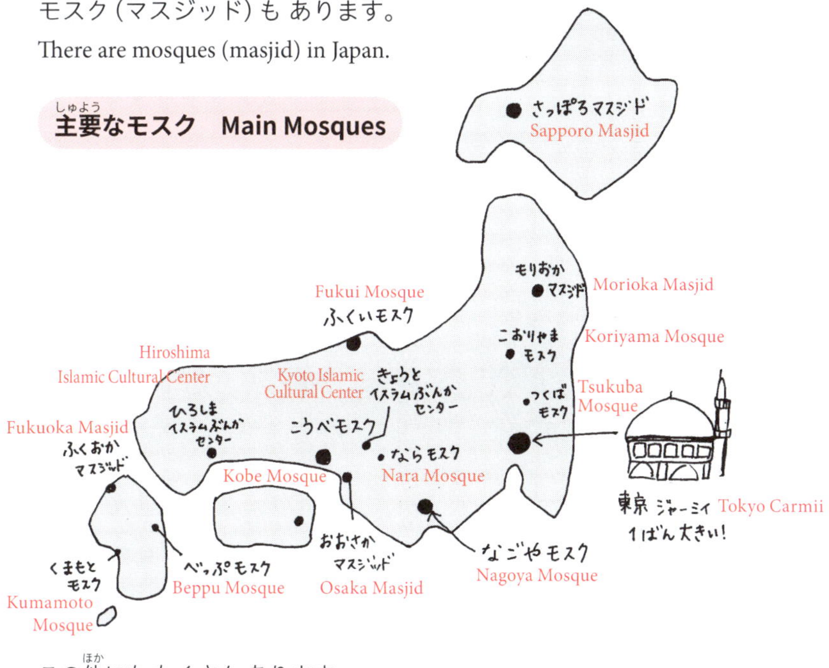

この他（ほか）にも たくさん あります。

Here are some more of the many mosques in Japan.

* http://islamjp.com/benri/indexen.htm

ムスリムの 人（ひと）の ための 便利（べんり）な サイト Some useful sites for Muslims
☞フードダイバーシティ（food diversity）：https://fooddiversity.today/id
☞ISLAMのホームページ：http://islamjp.com/

「だんだん」「どんどん」
dan dan versus *don don*

*https://matcha-jp.com/easy/7891

月曜日に、同僚（一緒に働いている人）の高橋さんが ラジープに 仕事を 頼みました。そして 金曜日に、高橋さんは ラジープに 仕事が どのくらい進んだか 聞いて、驚きました。どうしてでしょうか。

On Monday, Rajeep's co-worker Takahashi asked him to do a job. The following Friday, Rajeep informed Takahashi of his progress. Takahashi was shocked to hear how much Rajeep had done. Why was he shocked?

[Monday]
"Can I start working on this?"
"Sure, Let's do it *dondon* (quickly)!"

[Friday]
"How is it going, Rajeep?"
"I finished about 10%."

"What?!"
"After working Monday through Friday on it?!"
(only 10%)

"You said *dandan* (gradually), right?"
"I said *dondon*! (quickly)!"

「だんだん」と「どんどん」

dan dan and *don don*

だんだん *dan dan*

「だんだん」は「ゆっくり、すこしずつ」という 意味です。階段の 段が 語源です。
Dandan means "slowly" or "little by little." It is derived from the word for "stairs."

《例 Ex.》

だんだん 寒くなります。　It's slowly getting colder.

だんだん 日本語がじょうずになります。

You'll gradually get better at Japanese.

どんどん *don don*

「どんどん」は「ためらわないで する」という 意味です。兵隊行進の たいこの 音が 語源です。

Dondon means "without hesitation." It is derived from the sound of a soldier's marching drum.

《例 Ex.》

どんどん 行こう。　　　　Let's go quickly.

どんどん 食べてください。　Please eat a lot.

"It's progressing quickly!
About 90% complete!"

"Nice!"

日本の企業文化　Japanese Corporate Culture

まんがの 高橋さんは、ラジープの 先輩（長く 働いている 人）です。新しい 仕事を するときには、先輩や 上司に 仕事を はじめても いいか 聞きます。

In the manga, Takahashi is Rajeep's *senpai* (a person who has been working at the job longer). When beginning a new project, you have to ask your senpai or supervisor if you can start.

社長　CEO/President

副社長・専務
Executive Vice President / Senior Vice President

部長　Manager

課長・係長　Section Chief

一般社員　regular employee

＊会社によって 違います。　These can vary depending on the company.

上下関係　Relationship between superior and subordinate

日本では、上下関係が とても たいせつです。

In Japan, the relationship between superiors and subordinates is very important.

日本の 会社は 外国の 会社ほど カジュアルでは ありません。特に、上の 人と 話すときは 敬語（とても ていねいな ことば）を 使います。

Japanese companies are not as casual as foreign companies. People generally use *keigo* (honorific language), especially when speaking to their superiors.

先輩にも 敬語を 使います。
Keigo is also used with senpai.

朝礼　**Morning meetings**

いくつかの 会社は 朝礼が あります。たいてい 仕事の 連絡や 目標 などを 話します。

Some companies have morning meetings at which goals, reports, etc. are shared.

「ラジオ体操」という 3 分くらいの 短い 運動を する会社 (特に 工場) も あります。

Some companies (especially factories) conduct short stretching sessions that are about three minutes in length.

いんかん
印鑑　**Seals**

大切な 書類に サインを するときは、サインの となりに 印鑑が ひつようです。

When signing important documents, you have to affix your personal seal next to your signature.

↑ サイン Sign　　↑ 印鑑 Seal

社員は みんな ハンコを 持っています。ハンコは 文房具店や デパート、100円ショップや オンラインショップでも 買うことが できます。

All employees have their own *hanko*, an ink stamp that can be purchased at stationery shops, department stores, ¥100 shops, and online retailers.

外国人の ために ハンコを 作る 店も あります。カタカナや 漢字など、いろいろな デザインを 選ぶことが できます。

There are even shops that make stamps for foreigners. They offer a variety of designs such as *katakana* and *kanji*.

＊最近は、デジタルの 印鑑や クラウドサインも 人気です。

Recently, digital seals and cloud-based signatures have also become popular.

電話で 他の 会社の人や お客さんと 話すときには、敬語を 使わなければいけません。

When you speak on the phone with a client or another company, you have to use *keigo* (honorific language).

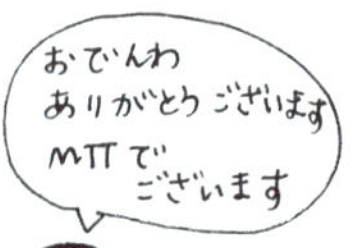

This is Rajeep from T. Tech. Thank you for your continued assistance.

Thank you for calling MTT.

ビジネスの 電話は「いつも 大変 お世話に なっております」か「お世話に なっております」を、名前の 後に 言います。「こんにちは」や「もしもし」、「元気ですか」は 言いません。

On business calls, use the formal expression (*itsumo*) *osewa ni natte orimasu* (roughly "I am (always) in your debt") after stating your name. Don't say *konnichiwa*, *moshimoshi*, or *genki desu ka*.

メールで In emails

差出人	Sender
宛先	Recipient
件名	Subject

鈴木様   Recipient's name

お世話になっております。T.Techのラジープです。

先日の〇〇の件ですが、□□□□□□□□□□□□□
□□□□□□□□□□□□□□□□□□□□□
□□□□□□□□□□□□□□□□□□□□□
□□□□□□□□□□□□□□□□□□□□□
□□□

Body

どうぞよろしくお願いいたします。
ラジープ   Sender's name

飲み会 Drinking parties

日本の 会社は、よく 飲み会を します。
飲み会の ときも、上下関係が 大切です。

Japanese companies often have drinking parties. A respectful attitude is important in these situations as well.

はじめに、上司が 話を して、かんぱい を します。

At the beginning of the party, the superior makes a small speech and a toast.

かんぱいの 前に、飲み物を 飲んだり、食べ物を 食べたりしては いけません。
You should not eat or drink before the toast is made.

お酌 Serving drinks

日本では お酌の 習慣が あります。下の 社員が 上の 人に お酌を します。お酌を するときは、瓶の ラベルが 見えるように します。

Japan has a custom for the serving of alcohol: lower-position employees serve alcohol to their superiors. When pouring, make sure the label is facing up.

飲み会の 終わり（しめ と 言います）に、みんなで 拍手を します。

At the end of the party (known as *shime*), all attendees clap their hands.

たいてい、幹事が「いよーおっ」と 言った後、リズミカルな 拍手を します。
Usually, the person in charge of the party will yell *iyo~*, after which everyone claps together in rhythm.

「ない」「いない」

nai versus inai

*https://matcha-jp.com/easy/8597

日本語の クラスで、スリが しんぱいそうなので、先生は「どうしましたか」 と聞きました。

In Japanese class, Suri seemed worried about something, so the teacher asked her, "What happened?"

"Ms. Suri, what happened?"

"Well… disappeared… (*inaku narimashita*)."

"Oh! Who?"
"Huh?"

"My pen."
"You mean you lost it… (*naku natta*)"

「ない」と「いない」

nai and *inai*

「ない」・「いない」 *nai* and *inai*

「ない」と「いない」は 同じ 意味です。しかし、「ない」は 物、「いない」は 人や 動物に 使います。

nai and *inai* have the same meaning. However, *nai* is used for inanimate things, while *inai* is used for animate things like people and animals.

ない・いない	例 Ex.		
ない *nai*	ペンが ない。 There is no pen.	財布が ない。 I don't have my wallet.	鍵が ない。 I don't see the key.
いない *inai*	先生が いない。 The teacher is away.	店の人が いない。 There's no staff.	ねこが いない。 I can't find my cat.

「なる」を使った 表現 Expressions using *naru* (to become)

ない＋なる → なくなる　　　いない＋なる → いなくなる

～なる	例 Ex.	
なくなる *naku naru*	ペンが なくなった。 The pen is gone.	財布が なくなった。 I lost my wallet.
いなくなる *inaku naru*	先生が いなくなった。 The teacher disappeared.	ねこが いなくなった。 The cat isn't here anymore.

"I lost my pen."

"Here it is!"

落とし物　Lost items

 **道で**　**On the street**

ちかくの 交番に 行って「〜を 落としました」と 言って ください。
Go to the nearest police box and say ~ *o otoshimashita* ("I lost ~ ").

警察官が 届出書を 書きます。落とした日、時間、落とした物の 形や 色を 伝えて ください。

"I lost my wallet!!"

The police officer will fill out a form for lost items. Tell the officer the date and time that the item was lost and other information such as the item's shape and color.

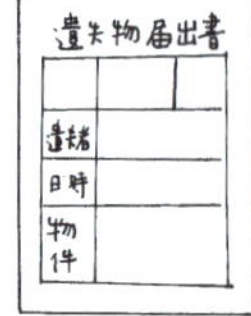

インターネットで 自分で 探すことも できます。
You can look for it yourself on the Internet.
＊https://www.npa.go.jp/bureau/soumu/ishitsubutsu/ishitsubutsulink.html

見つかったら、外国に 送ってもらうことも できます。送るために お金を 払わなければなりません。
If it is found, you can even ask them to send it to you overseas. You will have to pay the cost to ship it.

"We found it!"

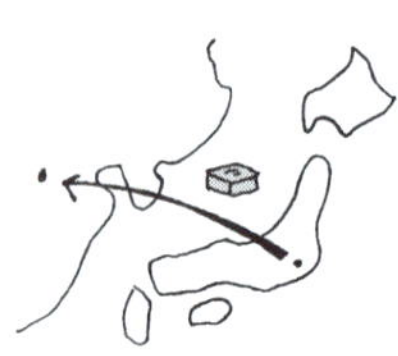

店で　At a store

てんいん　った
店員に 伝えてください。たいてい スーパーや デパートには サービスカウンター
　　　　　　　　　み　　　　　　　　　　　　　　　てんいん
が ありますが、見つからないときは、どの 店員でも だいじょうぶです。

Inform a shop attendant. Supermarkets and department stores usually have a service counter. If you can't find one, just speak with any store employee.

"Excuse me, I lost my smartphone."

"What type of smartphone?
What color is it?"

み　　　　　　　みせ　　れんらく　　　　　　　　　　と　　い　　　　　　　　　おく
見つかったら、店から 連絡が あります。「取りに 行きます」または「送ってくだ
　　　　　　った
さい」と 伝えてください。

If your lost item is found, the store will contact you. When they do, tell them either *tori ni ikimasu* ("I'll come get it") or *okutte kudasai* ("Please send it to me").

電車で　On the train

いえ　　　　　　　　ちか　　　　えき　　い　　　でん わ　えきいん　　わす もの　　　　　　き
家や ホテルの 近くに ある 駅に 行くか、電話で 駅員に 忘れ物が あるか 聞いてく
ださい。

Visit or call the station nearest your house or hotel and ask if your lost item has been found.

"Excuse me. I left my umbrella in the train."

"When?
Which line?"

落とし物は、見つけられたら、大きな 駅に 行きます。1〜2 週間後に、落とし物は 警察に 行きます。

When a lost item is found, it is sent to one of the main stations. After a week or two, it is then moved to a police station.

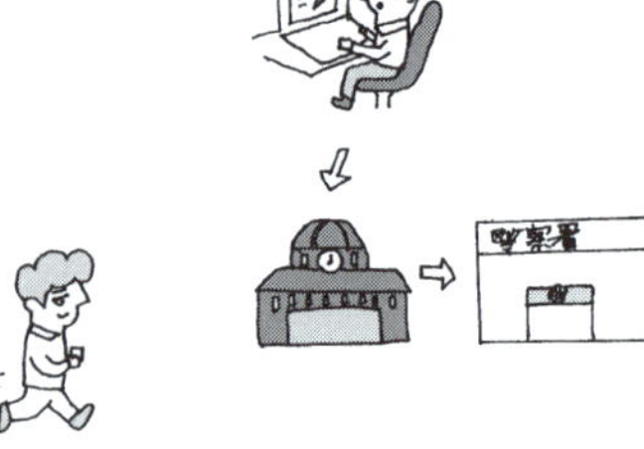

免許証、パスポートなど 身分 証明書を 持って、取りに 行ってください。

Bring some ID like your driver's license or passport and go get your item.

切符をなくしたとき If you lose your train ticket

駅員に 伝えて また お金を はらいます。

Tell the station worker and pay the fare again.

駅員が 再収受 証明書 という レシートを くれます。

The station worker will give you a receipt called *saishuuju shoumeisho*.

切符を 見つけた場合、再収受 証明書と 一緒に 駅に 持って 行ってください。お金を 返してもらえます。

If you find your ticket later, take it to the station. You can get a refund.

ICカードをなくしたとき **If you lose your IC card**

ICカードを 失（な）くしたときも、駅員（えきいん）に 伝（つた）えます。駅員（えきいん）が すぐに カードが 使（つか）えない ように します。

If you lose your IC card, tell a station worker. The worker will immediately deactivate your card so that it can't be used.

"I loaded it with ¥10,000."
"Don't worry."

新（あたら）しい ICカードを 作（つく）ったら、失（な）くした カードの 料金（りょうきん）が 入（はい）ります。

After your new IC card has been created, the money from your old card will be transferred.

手数料（てすうりょう）520円（えん）と 新（あたら）しい カードの デポジット 500円（えん）を 払（はら）います。その 500円（えん）は カードを 返（かえ）すときに 返（かえ）してもらえます。

You'll have to pay a service charge of ¥520 plus a ¥500 deposit for the new card. That deposit will be refunded when you return your IC card.

見（み）つけた、または拾（ひろ）ったとき **If you find or pick up an item**

店（みせ）の 人（ひと）や 警察（けいさつ）に 渡（わた）して ください。もし 3か月以上（げついじょう）、落（お）とした 人（ひと）が いない 場合（ばあい）、拾（ひろ）った 人（ひと）が もらうことが できます（クレジットカードや 身分証明書（みぶんしょうめいしょ）は もらえません）。

Please give it to a shop attendant or a police officer. If no one claims the item within three months, the person who found it can keep it (except for items like identification or credit cards).

「なにも」「なんでも」

nanimo versus *nandemo*

*https://matcha-jp.com/easy/9233

ラジープの 会社には、自動販売機が あります。同僚の 高橋さんが ラジープに 「なにか 飲みたいか」と 聞きました。ラジープは 飲み物が ほしかったのですが、高橋さんは、ラジープは 飲み物が ほしくない と 思ってしまいました。

The company where Rajeep works has a vending machine. His colleague Takahashi just asked him if he wants something to drink. Rajeep wants something to drink, but Takahashi thinks that he doesn't want anything.

"Want anything to drink? Some coffee or?"
"Nothing. (*nanimo*)"

"Really?"
"Right, nothing! "

"This is good!"

"Where's my drink?"
"What?"

「なにも」と「なんでも」
nanimo and *nandemo*

ラジープは「なにも」と 言いましたが、それは nothing の 意味です。Anything (is fine) と 言いたいときは「なんでも」と 言います。

Rajeep said *nanimo*, but that means "nothing" in this case. If he wants to respond "anything (is fine)," he should say *nandemo*.

➡ 「なにも」は いつも 否定形で 使います。

Nanimo is always used with a negative verb.

《例 Ex.》

なにも飲みません。　　　　　I won't drink anything.

➡ 「なんでも」は 英語で anything です。

The word *nandemo* means "anything" in English.

《例 Ex.》

なんでもいいです。　　　　　Anything is fine.

高橋さんのように Want something to drink? と 聞きたいときは、「なにか 飲む？」を 使います。

If you want to ask "Want something to drink?" like Takahashi does in the manga, say *nanika nomu?*

なにか 欲しいですか？　　　Do you want anything?

"Anything is fine."

"Anything is okay? Alright, I'll get you a coffee."

ほかの疑問詞 ＋ か / も / でも
Using か・も・でも with other indefinite pronouns

どこか / どこも / どこでも

I won't go anywhere today.

Would you like to go somewhere on Sunday?

Where?

Anywhere is fine!

だれか / だれも / だれでも

Is someone there?

There's no one here!

Help me! Anyone!

いつか / いつも / いつでも

I want to go to the US one day.

Please come anytime.

You are always funny.

You can eat any of them.

They all look good!
Is any one of them fine?

どちらか / どちらも / どちらでも

２つのときは どちら（どっち）を 使^{つか}います。「どっち」は くだけた 言^いいかたです。
When there are only two choices, *dochira* is used. *Docchi* is the more casual version.

Can I eat either of them?

You can eat either of them.

注^{ちゅう}！ Watch out!

1「いつも」「どれも」「どちらも（どっちも）」は 肯定^{こうてい}と 否定^{ひてい}の 両方^{りょうほう}に 使^{つか}えます。

* *Itsumo* and *doremo* can be used in both positive and negative sentences.

2 どこが、だれが、いつが、どれが、どちらが 「か」では ありません。気^きをつけてください。

* Be careful: When asking questions, the か becomes が.

Which would you like (hot or ice)?

Hot please.

自動販売機　Vending machines

ラジープの 同僚 の 高橋さんは、会社の 自動販売機で 飲み物を 買って いました。日本には、どこでも 自動販売機が あります。ほとんどは、飲み物の 自動販売機です。たいていは、現金だけではなく、IC カードや スマートフォンでも 買うことが できます。

Rajeep's colleague Takahashi was buying drinks from a vending machine at the office. In Japan, you can find vending machines everywhere. Most of them contain drinks. You can usually make purchases with an IC card or your smartphone instead of cash, if you prefer.

食券機　Food-ticket machines

高速道路の サービスエリアや フードコート、小さな ラーメン屋などには、食べ物の チケットを 買う機械も あります。

You can also find food-ticket machines at highway rest areas, food courts, and some small ramen shops.

買いかた *Making a purchase*

1. お金を 入れる
   Insert the money

2. 料理を 選ぶ
   Select your dish

3. 店の人に チケットを 渡す
   Give your ticket(s) to an employee

4. 番号札か チケットの 半分、または 機械を もらう
   Take your number, ticket stub, or device

5. 水や 箸、スプーンなどを 用意する
   Prepare your water, chopsticks, spoon, etc.

6. 食べ物を 取りに 行く
   Pick up your food

タッチパネルの 食券機も あります。いろいろな 言語を 選べますし、食べ物の 写真も 見ることが できます。それに、Visa カードや スマートフォンアプリで 買うこともできます。

There are food-ticket machines with touch screens, too. They have a selection of languages and display pictures of the dishes. You can also buy tickets with a Visa card or smartphone app.

はな

hana

*https://matcha-jp.com/easy/7490

日本語には、同じ 音の ことばが たくさん あります。たとえば「雨」と「飴」、「橋」と「箸」などです。生け花の 先生は「はな」と 言いました。クリスティーヌは「花」だ と 思いましたが、ちがうようです。

Many Japanese words have the same pronunciation but different meanings. For example, *ame* can mean either "rain" or "candy," while *hashi* can refer to a "bridge" or "chopsticks." Here, the flower-arrangement instructor said the word *hana*. Christine thought she meant "flower," but it seems that the teacher had a different meaning in mind.

"This flower (*hana*) is…"

"Achoo!"

"My nose (*hana*) is *muzumuzu*."
"*Muzumuzu*…?"

"The flower is itchy?"

「花」と「鼻」

hana (flower) and *hana* (nose)

「はな」には２つの 意味が あります。

The word *hana* has two meanings.

日本語	英語
花	flower
鼻	nose

日本語の 発音 (言うときの 音) は 同じです。
「花」か「鼻」か、どちらか わからないときは、たいてい 文脈 (文の意味) や 状況 で わかります。
また、よく 花には「お」を つけて「お花」と 言うので、鼻ではないと わかるでしょう。

These words have the same pronunciation. When people don't know which meaning is intended, they generally just consider the context or situation to understand.

Also, people often attach the prefix *o* when talking about flowers (*o-hana*) to make it clear that they are not talking about a nose.

"My nose is itchy."

"Do you have allergies? Are you okay?"

ピッチアクセント　Pitch accents

花と 鼻は、発音だけではなく、アクセントも 同じです。どちらも 平らです。
The words for flower and nose have not only the same pronunciation but also the same
accent (flat in both cases). There are many words like this that have the same pronunciation
but different meanings.

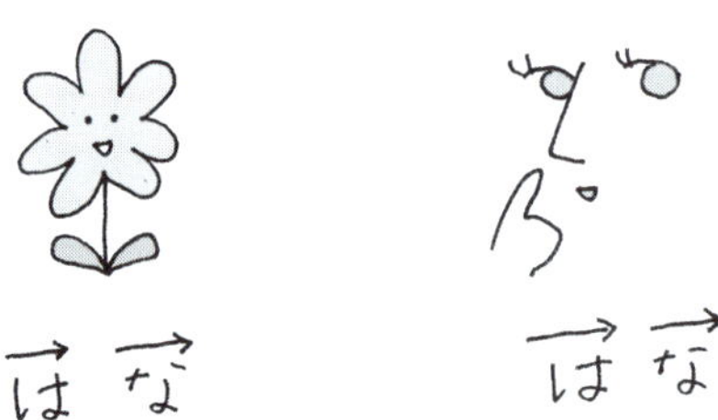

しかし、いくつかの 言葉は、ピッチアクセント（音の 高低）で 意味が 変わります。
In some words, however, the pitch accent changes to indicate which of the words is being
expressed.

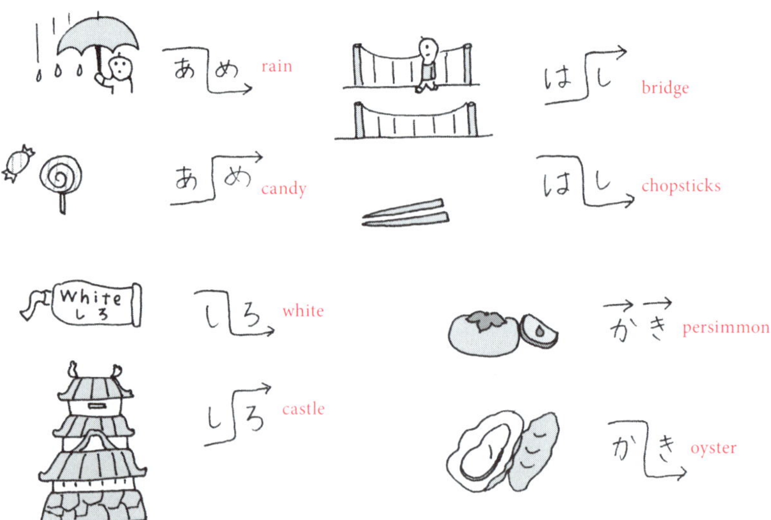

いろいろな地方のアクセント　Regional accents

地方によって、アクセントが 変わります。たとえば、大阪や 京都などの 関西地方は アクセントが 東京の 標準語と 反対に なることが よくあります。

Pitch accents depend on the region. For instance, accents in the Kansai region (such as those in Osaka and Kyoto) are often the opposite of the standard Tokyo accent.

たとえば、雨は、東京では「あ」が 高いですが、京都や 大阪では「め」が 高いようです。また、東京の 北のほうの 地方では、アクセントが あまり ありません。

In Tokyo, for example, the あ in あめ (meaning "rain") is emphasized, while people from Kyoto and Osaka tend to stress the め. Also, the region to the north of Tokyo has no clearly defined accent.

いろいろな アクセントが ありますが、日本語を 話すとき、アクセントを 心配しないで くださいね。

There are a lot of different accents, but you don't need to worry about them when you speak Japanese.

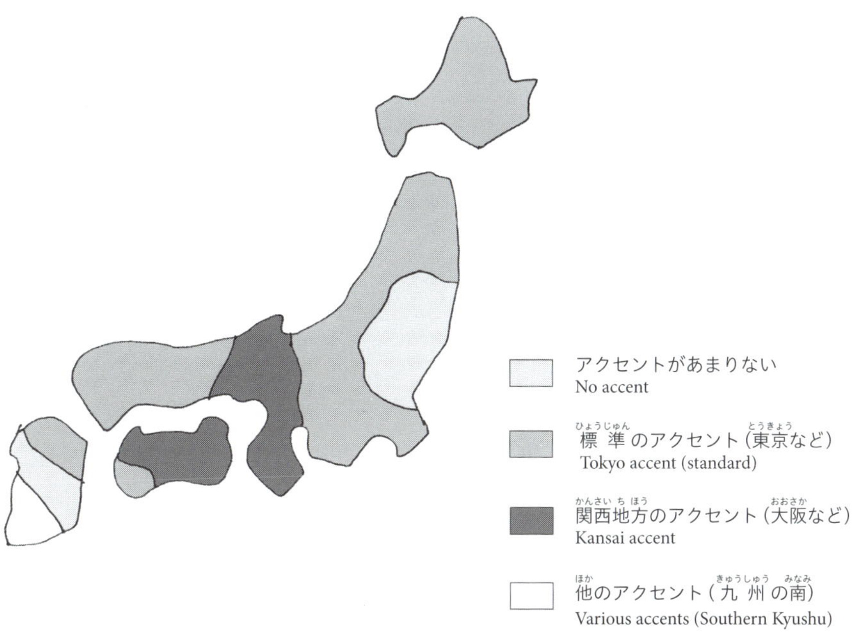

方言 Dialects

アクセントだけではなく、地方によって いろいろな ことばと 表現が ちがいます。

In addition to accents, some words and expressions vary depending on the region.

例：わからない（I don't understand）

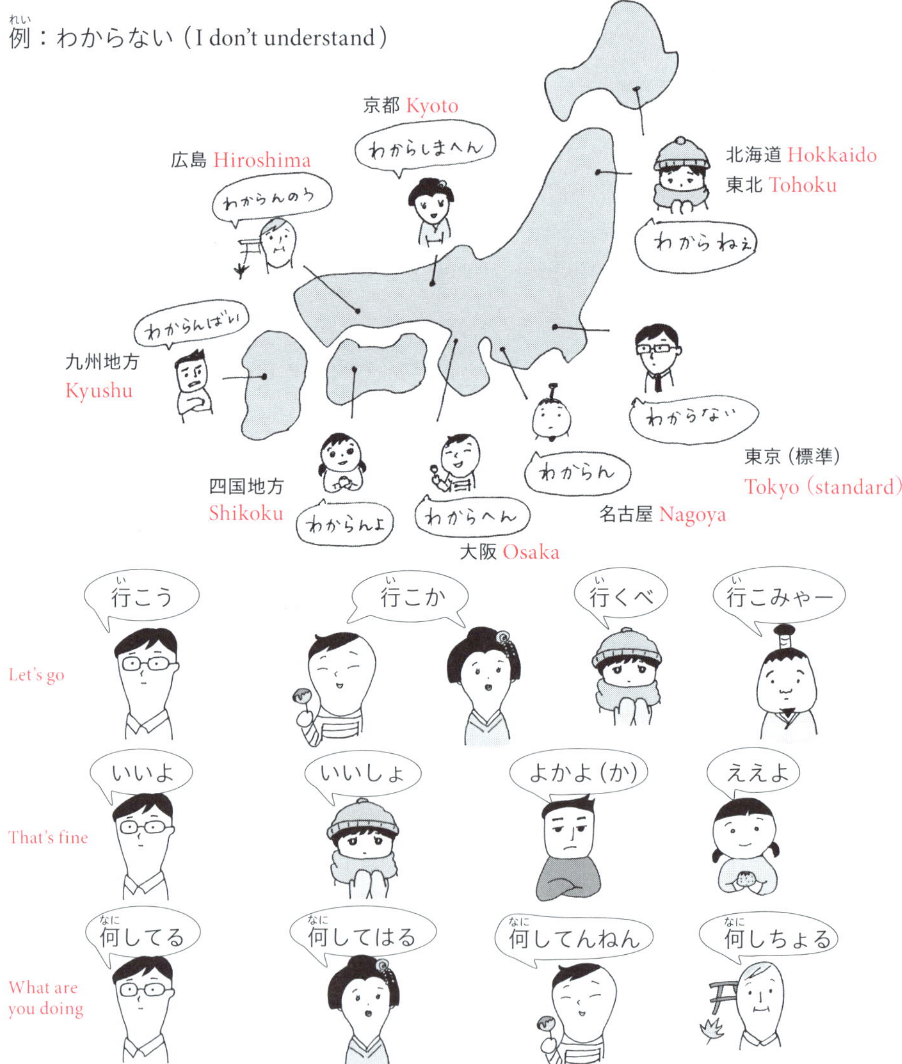

＊他にも いろいろな 方言が あります。また 同じ 地方でも 町によって 表現が 変わります。

There are other dialects, too. Also, each town in a region can have its own unique expressions.

とうきょう 東 京 Tokyo

How much?

Just ¥1,000 is fine.

Really?

おおさか 大阪 Osaka

How much?

Just ¥500 is fine.

Really?

とうきょう 東 京 Tokyo

What are you doing?

I'm going to a café.

Sounds good!

きゅうしゅう 九 州 Kyushu

What are you doing?

I'm going to the ramen shop.

Sounds good!

クリスティーヌは、電車で いけばなの レッスンに 行きます。電車の中で、いつも 日本語を 勉強 しています。「〜そう」という 表現を 見つけたので、さっそく 使ってみました。

Christine takes the train when going to her ikebana lessons. She always studies Japanese on the train. She found the expression ~sou ("looks" or "sounds") and wants to use it right away.

"looks delicious…
sounds fun… "

"This will be cute if we cut it."
"If we cut it, it looks pitiful. (*kawaisou*)"

"Not pitiful."

"I think it is pitiful!"
"Okay…"

～そう
looks, sounds

い-形容詞は「い」が「そう」に なります。な-形容詞は「そう」を つける だけです。

With i-adjectives, change the final *i* to *sou*. For na-adjectives, just add *sou* to the end.

い-形容詞　i-adjectives	な-形容詞　na-adjectives
楽し**そう**　sounds fun	元気**そう**　looks well
おもしろ**そう**　sounds interesting	しずか**そう**　sounds quiet
おいし**そう**　looks delicious	べんり**そう**　sounds convenient
暑**そう**　looks hot	しんせつ**そう**　looks kind

しかし、「かわいい」は「かわいそう」に なると、pitiful という 意味に なります。ですから、looks cute / sounds cute と 言うときは、「かわいい と おもいます」と 言いましょう。

However, when *kawaii* becomes *kawaisou*, the meaning changes to "pitiful." If you want to say "looks/sounds cute," you can say *kawaii to omoimasu*.

"Seems like it will be cute if we cut it."

"Yes, I think so too."

おいしそう VS. おいしいそう
oishisou versus *oishiisou*

「〜そう」は、とても にている 表現が あるので、気をつけてください。

The expressions using *sou* are very similar, so watch out!

「い」が 変わりません。誰かから 聞きました という 意味に なります。な-形容詞 は、「だそう」を つけます。

The *i* doesn't change, so the expression refers to something the speaker heard from someone else. For na-adjectives, add *dasou*.

It looks delicious!

It's supposed to be delicious (according to the guidebook).

Looks interesting!

I heard this is interesting. The teacher told me.

I returned from my trip.　You look well.

I heard my dad is doing well.　Good!

 〜 *mitai*

くだけた会話では「みたい」を よく 使います。見たときや、聞いたときの 感じを 表します。でも、使いかたが すこし 違うので 気をつけてください。

In casual conversations, the word *mitai* is used often. It indicates how something appeared to the speaker when they saw or heard it.

Noun ＋ みたい

This cat looks like a pig!

Verb ＋ みたい

It seems he got upset.

形容詞のときは、「おいし**い**そう」「元気**だ**そう」と 同じ 使いかたです。

It is used the same way as おいしいそう and 元気だそう.

い-形容詞　i-adjectives

おいしいみたい

It seems delicious.

な-形容詞　na-adjectives

元気みたい

It seems (someone) is well.

〜よう　〜*you*

フォーマルな 場面では「よう」を 使います。

The word *you* is suitable for formal situations.

Looks like it will be sunny tomorrow.

生け花（華道）　Ikebana (kado)

いけばなは、日本の 伝統的な 花の アレンジ（いけかた）です。空間が 大切です。

Ikebana is the Japanese tradition of arranging flowers. Empty space is important.

線も 大切なので、枝を よく 使います。花は たくさん 使いません。

The lines are also important, so branches are often used to shape them. Not a lot of flowers are used.

西洋の フラワーアレンジメントは 花を たくさん 使います。

By comparison, Western flower arrangements use a lot of flowers.

生け花は すこし 枯れた 葉と 花も 使います。

In *ikebana*, slightly wilted leaves and flowers are used too.

剣山 という 針を 使います。

Ikebana arrangements are assembled on a *kenzan*, a base that contains sharp pins.

外国で 有名な 盆栽は、おじいさんたちに 人気です。

Bonsai trees, which are well-known in foreign countries, are popular with older men.

若い 人たちは、盆栽よりも 苔玉を 部屋の 中に 置くほうが 好きです。

Young people prefer decorating their rooms with *kokedama* rather than bonsai.

その他の伝統文化　Other cultural traditions

茶道 *Tea ceremony*

抹茶の 淹れかたと 飲みかたの マナーを 学びます。

Learning the rites for serving and drinking matcha

書道 *Calligraphy*

筆を 使って 字を 書きます。

Writing kanji with a brush

三味線 *Shamisen*・琴 *Koto*・和太鼓 *Wadaiko*

三味線は お座敷、琴は お正月、和太鼓は お祭りのときに 主に 演奏します。

Shamisen are mainly performed in tatami rooms during parties, koto are for the New Year holiday, and wadaiko are played during festivals.

柔道 *Judo*・剣道 *Kendo*・弓道 *Kyudo*

日本の 伝統的な ものには よく「道」を 使います。もともと 武士（侍） の 生きかた（武士道）から きました。道は、way, path の 意味です。結果より、その道を 行くことが 大切です。

Traditional Japanese activities often end with the kanji 道 (*do*). This concept originates from 武士道 (*bushido*), which were rules for how samurai should live and act. The character 道 means "way" or "path," emphasizing that the journey is more important than the end result.

「きれい」「きらい」

kirei versus *kirai*

*https://matcha-jp.com/easy/7226

クリスティーヌは、いけばな展へ 行きました。クリスティーヌは すばらしい いけばなを 見て、先生に 自分の 気持ちを 伝えました。でも、先生は とても びっくり して、かなしそうです。どうしてでしょうか。

Christine went to an exhibit for the Japanese art of flower arrangement. She tries to express her feelings to her teacher while looking at the fantastic works. But her teacher was very surprised and looked sad. Why was that?

"Welcome to the flower arrangement exhibition."

"I hate flowers!"
"Oh!"

"This is scary."
"I hate that too."

"Oh, what's wrong…?"

「きらい」と「こわい」

kirai and *kowai*

日本語には、発音が にている ことばが あります。「きれい」と「きらい」、「かわいい」と「こわい」は、にています。でも、意味は 全然 違いますから、気をつけ なければなりません。

Japanese has similar-sounding words such as *kirei* and *kirai* and *kawaii* and *kowai*. But they have totally different meanings, so you need to be careful when using them.

日本語	意味
きれい	beautiful
きらい	dislike
かわいい	pretty; cute
こわい	scary

「きれい」は「きれえ」、「かわいい」は「かわいー」と 発音したほうが いいです。

You are better off pronouncing *kirei* like きれえ and *kawaii* as かわいー.

"Those are beautiful!
  This is cute!"

"Thanks."

にていることば　Similar Words

きれい　Pretty, Clean

「きれい」は、２つの 意味が あります。

The word *kirei* has two meanings.

花が きれい

The flower is pretty.

ぼくの 手は きれい

My hands are clean.

かわいい　Cute

「かわいい」は 子どもや 小さいものだけでは ありません。

Kawaii is not only for describing kids or small things.

いろいろな 物や 人を かわいい と言います。

People use *kawaii* to describe many different people and things.

キャラ

character or mascot

メイドカフェ

maid café

原宿＊の ロリータファッション

lolita fashion in Harajuku＊

＊原宿は かわいい 文化で 有名な ところです。
Harajuku is a famous place in *kawaii* culture.

こわかわいい	こわい	＋ かわいい	scary and cute
やみかわいい	病みます	＋ かわいい	sick and cute

暗い スタイルも 「かわいい」 と 言う 人たちが います。

Some people even call goth styles *kawaii*.

＊ https://matcha-jp.com/jp/3081

ほめることば Compliments and words of praise

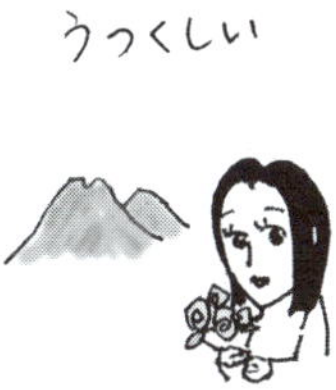
うつくしい

beautiful

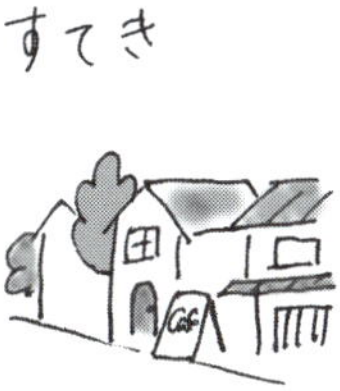
すてき

nice; lovely

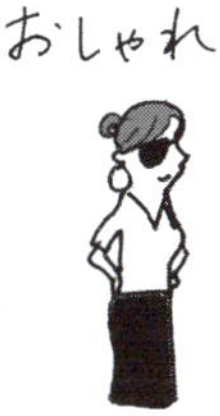
おしゃれ

stylish

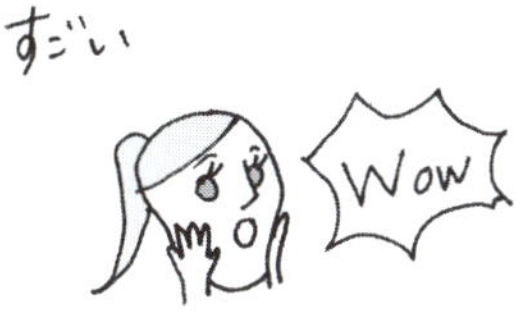
すごい
Wow

wow

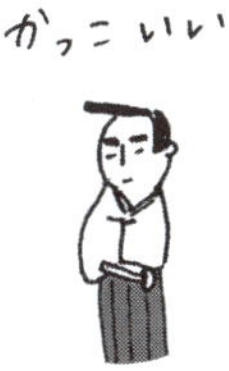
かっこいい

cool

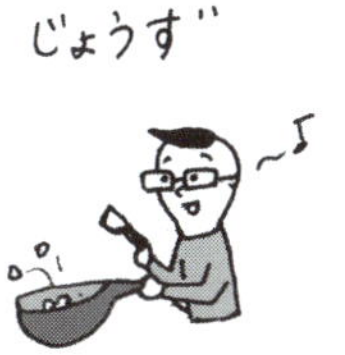
じょうず

good or skillful

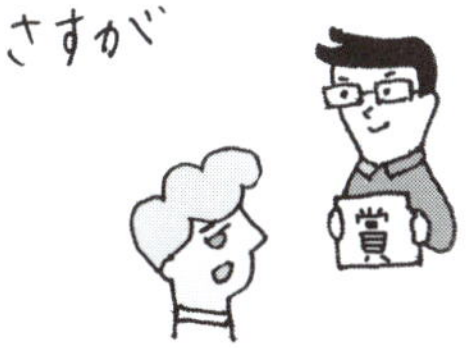
さすが
賞

as I expected (you're great)

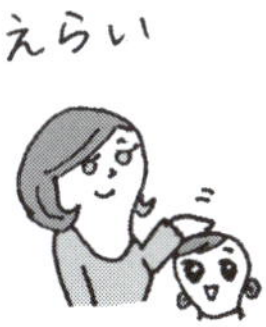
えらい

good job

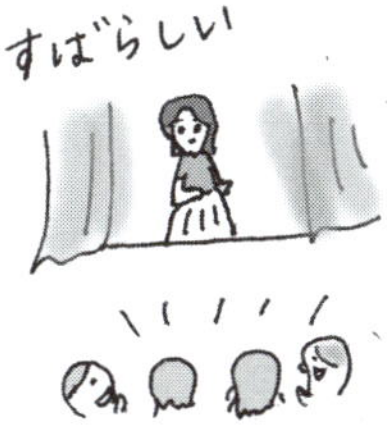
すばらしい

wonderful; fantastic

⇨ ほめられたとき When receiving compliments

日本人は たいてい 「いえいえ」「そんなことないです」「まだまだです」 と 言います。
Japanese usually respond to compliments with "no no," "that's not true," or " I'm not there yet."

やまださんは すばらしいです！
いえいえ

にほんごが じょうずですね
いいえ まだまだです

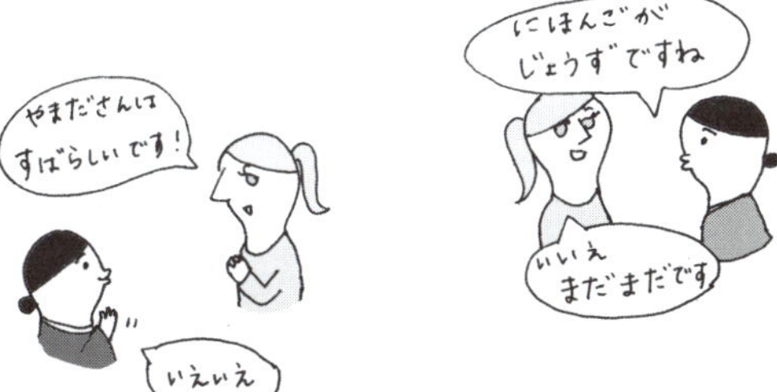

日本人の美意識　Japanese aesthetics

日本人は「変わっていくもの」「終わるもの」「完ぺきじゃないもの」を美しいと思います。

Japanese people find beauty in things changing or ending as well as things that are imperfect.

少し枯れている葉
虫が食べた葉

slightly wilted leaves
leaves eaten by insects

散っていく桜

falling cherry blossoms

古い湯のみ

old tea cups

日本人は季節が変わるのを楽しみます。

Japanese people enjoy the changing of the seasons.

季節のあいさつ

seasonal greetings

月見

moon-viewing party

古いものが好きですが、清潔にすることを大切にしています。

While Japanese people like old things, cleanliness is also important to them.

家に入るときは靴をぬぎます。洗濯ものや布団を外に干すのは、はずかしくありません。清潔なかんじがします。

When Japanese people enter a house, they take off their shoes to keep the floors clean. They aren't embarrassed by hanging clothes or blankets outside, as they consider this a sign of cleanliness.

人 People

男 の人は、筋肉ムキムキな 人より、やさしそうな 人や まじめそうな 人
が 人気です。 女 の人は、セクシーな 人より かわいくて 元気な 人が 人気
です。

In the case of men, appearing kind and responsible is preferable to being muscular. For women, a cute and cheerful appearance is more preferred than looking sexy.

また、メガネ男子(メガネを かけている 男 の人)も 人気です。 女 の人
は、顔は 小さく、目は 大きく なりたいので、写真を 加工する(変える)
人が 多いです。

Also, *meganedanshi* (men who wear glasses) are trendy. Many women want to have small faces and big eyes, so they retouch their pictures using filters.

日本では、シャイな 人や ひかえめな 人が 好まれます。(好む＝好き)

In Japan, people who are shy or humble are well-liked.

さわやか、せいけつな ファッションが 人気です。

Fresh and clean fashion is popular.

まんがのことば
Speech style of manga

*https://matcha-jp.com/easy/7599

インドネシアで、日本の まんがは とても 人気が あります。
スリも、まんがが 大好きです。とくに、少年（男の子）まんがを よく読みます。ある日、日本語の クラスで、スリが 話したとき、先生は おどろきました。

In Indonesia, Japanese comics are very popular. Suri likes them too, especially *shonen manga* (comics for boys). One day, she says something in Japanese that surprises her teacher.

"Where are you from, Ms. Suri?"

"Bandon!
You know that?!"

"Ms. Suri, you shouldn't say *shitteru ka*."

"But in manga…"

「か？」をつけた しつもん
Questions using *ka*?

少 年 まんがでは、普通形の 後に 「か？」を つけることが よく あります。

In *shonen manga*, the plain form of a verb is often followed by the particle か.

じしょけい dictionary form	「か？」をつけた しつもん question with *ka*?
見る　to see	見たか？　You see it?
行く　to go	行ったか？　You went?

強い 言いかたですから、少 年 まんがでは、男 の人が よく 使います。でも、普通 の 生活で 使うと、そのことばを 聞いた 人は 「らんぼうだ」と 思うかもしれません。しつもんを するときは、「ますか？」や 「ですか？」と 言いましょう。

These expressions sound very forceful and rough, so they are often used by male characters in shonen manga. If you use them in the real world, people might think you are a rough or rude person. When asking a question, say *masu ka* or *desu ka*.

"I'm from Bandon.
Do you know of it?"

"Yes.
I know it."

いろいろな話しかた　The different styles of speech

 Politeness level

くだけた話しかた　casual　→　ていねい　polite　→　敬語　formal

"Want some?"
"Yeah"

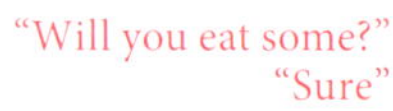

"Will you eat some?"
"Sure"

"Would you like some?"
"Yes, please"

くだけた話しかた	ていねいな話しかた	敬語（尊敬語）honorific	敬語（謙譲語）humble
ありがと thank you	ありがとうございます	(self only)	どうもありがとうございます
ごめん I'm sorry	すみません	(self only)	申し訳ございません
わかんない I don't understand	わかりません	おわかりになりません	わかりかねます
する to do	します	なさいます	いたします
いく to go	いきます	いらっしゃいます	まいります
みる to see	みます	ご覧になります	拝見します

In writing

学校の 論文や 仕事の レポートなどを 書くときは、「〜のだ」「〜である」「〜だろうか」を よく 使います。

When writing things like school papers and work reports, the endings *noda*, *de aru*, and *darou ka* are used often.

When speaking

話すときは、「だよね」「〜の？」などを 文の 終わりに よく 使います。特に、「〜ね」は 同意（同じ 気持ち）を あらわすので 大切です。ときどき「〜さ」「〜さぁ」を 使う人も いますが、これには 意味がありません。

＊話しかたは 地方によっても 違います。

Endings such as *dayone* and ~*no*? are used regularly when speaking. In particular, ~*ne* is very important because it indicates agreement (that you feel the same way). Some people also end sentences with ~*sa* or ~*saa*, but these are filler words that don't carry any meaning.

* Different geographical areas often have distinct speaking styles.

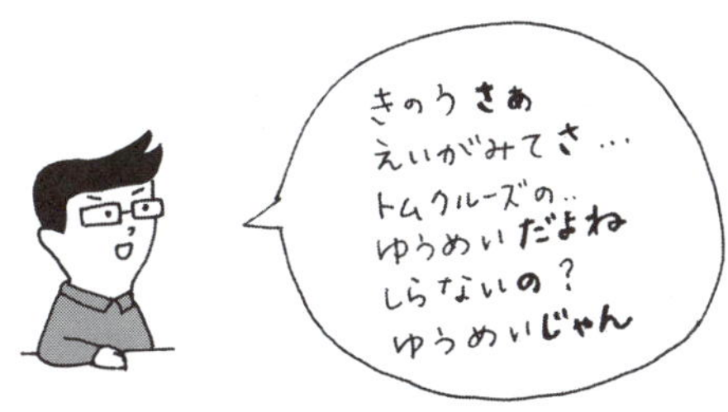

まんがのキャラクター
Characters in manga (Japanese comics)

まんがでは、話しかたの ちがいが わかりやすいです。下は、ぜんぶ 同じ 文ですが、話しかたが ちがいます。

Manga clearly demonstrates the different styles of speech. The sentences below all convey the same meaning, but the style of each is different.

男の子　boy

女の子　girl

チャラ男　shallow playboy

ギャル　flirtatious party girl

まじめ、つめたい　serious, cold

お嬢様　feminine and snobbish

他にも、おじいちゃん、おばあちゃんの キャラクターは 「〜じゃのう」、侍の キャラクターは 「〜でござる」を、よく 使います。

Aside from these, elderly characters often use *~janou*, and samurai say *~de gozaru*.

⇨ まんがの 例を 見てみましょう！
Let's take a look at some examples from manga.

礼儀正しい店員とお嬢様

A **polite** store employee and a **feminine** lady

いかがいたしますか？
How may I help you?

そうねぇ　こちらの お店は 何が おすすめかしら？
Yes…what do you recommend here?

男らしい先輩とギャル風OL

A **masculine** senior employee and
a **flirtatious** secretary

先輩！　お疲れ様でぇーす
Hey Senpai! *Otsukaresama de-su* (literally "you've
worked hard").

おう　おつかれー
Hey, you too~

おじいちゃん

An **elderly** man

そうじゃのう
Yes…

昔っから 婆さんは 優しいからのう
Your grandmother has always been kind.

「〜ませんか」「〜ましょうか」

masen ka versus mashou ka

*https://matcha-jp.com/easy/7340

林は、駅で 大きい 荷物を 持っている おばあさんを 見ました。林は おばあさんを 手伝いたい と思いました。でも……。

At the station, Rin sees an old lady carrying a heavy-looking bag. He wants to help her, but…

"So heavy…?"

"Huh!"
"Won't you help? (*tetsudai masen ka*?)"

"What help? Me?"
"Yes!"

"I can't carry more than this…"
"Won't you carry some baggage?"

「〜ませんか」 と 「〜ましょうか」

masen ka and *mashou ka*

「〜ませんか」 は、相手が したいか どうかを 聞くときに 使います。いっしょに なにか したいときも 使います。「〜ましょうか」 は、手伝いたいときに 使います。

The ending *masen ka* is used when asking if the other party wants to do something or not, so it can be used for inviting them to do an activity. Conversely, *mashou ka* is used for offering your help.

	英語	例 Ex.
〜ませんか	Would you like to 〜 ?	家に 来ませんか。 Would you like to come to my house? いっしょに 飲みませんか。 Would you like to get some drinks together?
〜ましょうか	Shall I 〜 ?	荷物を 持ちましょうか。 Shall I carry (your) baggage? 窓を 開けましょうか。 Shall I open the window (for you)?

"Shall I help with those?"

"Ah, thank you."

荷物　Nimotsu

飛行機の 中に 持っていく 小さい 荷物は、「てにもつ」です。大きい 荷物は、空港 で あずけるので、「あずけにもつ」です。

The small luggage you bring onto an airplane is *tenimotsu*. The large luggage you check in (*azukeru*) is called *azukenimotsu*.

宅配便や 郵便局から 送る物 も、「にもつ」と 言います。

Packages that are sent through a delivery service or post office are also called *nimotsu*.

会社で、まじめに 仕事を しない人も 「おにもつ」と 呼ばれます。

A company employee who doesn't work hard is called *o-nimotsu*.

大きい荷物をあずけたいとき　When storing large luggage items

1 ホテル　Hotel

たいていの ホテル*では、チェックアウトした後でも、少しの 時間、荷物を あずけることが できます。

At most hotels*, you can leave your luggage for a short time even after you check out.

*ホテルによって ちがいます。ホテルの人に 聞いてください。

This can vary, so you should check if your hotel offers this service.

あずける　leave
あずかる　keep

2 ロッカー　Locker

大きい 駅や デパートには ロッカーが あります。たいてい 一日 300円 (小) から 800円 (大) です。硬貨だけでなく、IC カードも 使えます。英語、中国語、韓国語の タッチパネルも あります。

Large stations and department stores have lockers. These typically cost ¥300 (a small locker) to ¥800 (a big locker) per day. Aside from coins, you can also pay with your IC card. Some touch panels offer menus in English, Chinese, and Korean.

また 東京駅には、いくつか 手荷物あずかりサービスの 場所が あります。

In addition, Tokyo Station has several locations for baggage storage.

*http://www.tokyostationcity.com/en/information/locker.html

3 アプリ　Apps

荷物を あずける 場所を 見つける アプリも あります。これも 英語、中国語、韓国語が あります。

There are even some apps that will direct you to places for storing your luggage. These are available in the English, Chinese, and Korean languages as well.

*https://cloak.ecbo.io/en

*https://www.dantai-ryokou.com/kankonews/page_6060.html

電車に乗るときのマナー　Manners on the train

でんしゃに 乗るときは、並んで、おりる 人を 待ちます。

Wait in line to board until people on the train get off.

満員電車 (人が たくさんの 電車) で、ドアの 近くに いるときは、後ろの 人の ために 一度おりて、また 戻ります。

If you are standing by the door on a crowded train, exit once so people behind you can get off, then reboard the train.

エスカレーターでは、みんなが 左側 (大阪は 右側) に 立ちます。急いでいる 人が エスカレーターを 歩くからです。しかし、歩くのは 危ないので、歩かないでください。

When riding an escalator, people stand on the left side (or the right side if in Osaka). This is because people who are in a hurry walk up the other side of the escalator. Walking on a moving escalator is dangerous, though, so please don't do that!

大きい 音
loud sounds

大きい 声
loud voice

大きい 荷物を
席に おく
placing large belongings
on the seat

大きい 着信音
loud ringtones

お酒を 飲む
drinking alcohol

足を ひろげる
stretching out legs

化粧を する
putting on makeup

イチャイチャする
making out

上の絵に ある 悪い マナーの ほかに、においの 強い 食べ物を 食べるのも よく ありません。ガムや 小さい お菓子は 食べても いいです。

In addition to the poor manners depicted in the above drawing, eating strong-smelling food is also not good. Gum, small snacks, and sweets are okay.

新幹線や、観光の ための 電車は 食べ物を 食べても だいじょうぶです。駅弁（駅で 売っている 弁当）には、地元の 名物が あるので、人気です。

Eating meals is fine on the *shinkansen* or sightseeing trains. *Ekiben* (*bento* boxes sold at stations) are popular because they contain famous local ingredients and cuisine.

「助けて」「手伝って」
tasukete versus tetsudatte

*https://matcha-jp.com/easy/8677

いけばなの レッスン中、クリスティーヌが「助けてください」と 言ったので、先生は びっくり しました。どうして 先生は、びっくり したのでしょうか？

During her ikebana lesson, Christine said *tasukete kudasai*, which shocked her teacher. Why was her teacher shocked?

"Oh, my… Save me please…"

"OH!"　"The flowers…"

"What happened?"

"There are so many. It's hard to pick."

"You startled me…"

「助けて」と「手伝って」

tasukete and *tetsudatte*

日本語には「to help」の ことばが 2つ あります。「助ける」と「手伝う」です。

Japanese has two verbs for "to help": *tasukeru* and *tetsudau*.

助ける

病気、災害から 救う

助けるの 漢字は 力 が あります。

Tasukeru is used when saving someone from a serious illness or rescuing someone during an emergency. Its kanji 助 contains the radical for power (力).

《例 Ex.》

つなみのとき、人を 助けた。　I saved some people during the tsunami.

手伝う

人の 仕事を いっしょに してあげる

手伝うの 漢字は 手が あります。

Testudau is used when helping someone do something. The kanji 手 means "hand".

《例 Ex.》

お母さんの 料理を 手伝った。　I helped Mom cook.

花を 選ぶときには「手伝ってください」を 使ったほうが いいですね。

When asking for help with selecting flowers, you should say *tetsudatte kudasai*.

"Can you help me pick out some flowers?"

"Sure, I'll help you."

どちらを使う？　Which should I use?

「助ける」と「手伝う」のように、1つの 英語の ことばに、いくつかの 日本語の 訳が ある場合は、気をつけてください。

As with *tasukeru* and *tetsudau*, think carefully about which Japanese translation is appropriate when there are several possibilities.

変更・変化・改革・お釣り　Change

予定を 変更する
change a plan

色が 変化する
color changes

世界を 改革したい
want to change the world

お釣りを もらう
receive change (after paying)

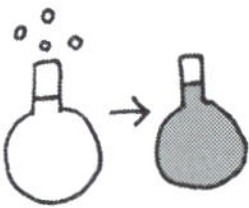

帰る・戻る・返す　Return

家に 帰る
return home for the day

同じ ところに 戻る
return to the same place

本を 返す
return a book

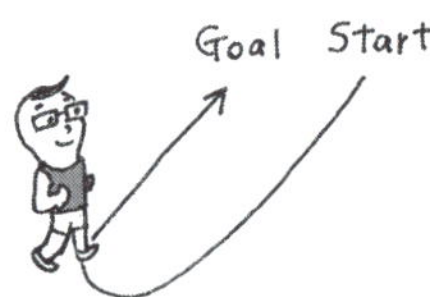

泊まる・いる　Stay

ホテルに 泊まる
stay at a hotel

家に いる
stay at home

冷たい・寒い　Cold

冷たい 食べ物と 飲み物
cold food and drink

今日は 寒い
It's cold today.

見る・会う　See

鳥を 見る
see (watch) a bird

友達に 会う
see (meet) a friend

自由・無料/ただ・ひま　Free

自由に なる
become free

無料/ただの 飲み物
a free drink

ひまです
I'm free (not busy).

＊「無料」と「ただ」は 同じ 意味です。　*Muryou* and *tada* have the same meaning.

命・生活・人生　Life

新しい 命
a new life

毎日の 生活
everyday life

人の 人生
human life

記号　Symbols

記号も 意味と 使いかたが ちがうので、気をつけてください。

Symbols also have different meanings and usages you should be aware of.

二重丸	丸	三角	ばつ
◎	○	△	×
とても いい	いい	まあまあ	よくない
very good	good	acceptable	not good

遠くに いる人に「だいじょうぶ」と 言いたいとき
には、手で 大きな ○を 作ります。

When you want to tell a person far away that "it's okay,"
make a big circle with your arms.

また、日本人は OK を Good の 意味でも 使います。

The word "okay" also means "good" to Japanese people.

テストの ときも、正しい 答えには ○を 書きます。答えが 正しくないときには、
✔を 書きます。

○ is used to mark correct answers on a test. When answers are incorrect, they are marked
with ✔.

～（から）

9：00～5：00　　9時 から 5時　　From 9 o'clock to 5 o'clock.

日本では「～」を 使います。これは 英語の「-」と 同じように 使います。

Japanese use the ～ symbol in a similar way to the English en dash (–).

また、長い 言葉を 省略する(言わない)ときや、例を 言うときも、～を 使います。
「～」は、「なになに」と 言います。

The ～ symbol is also used when omitting a long word or phrase or when giving an example. It is pronounced *naninani*.

～する　　　　I will do ＿＿＿＿＿＿.
naninani suru

日本人が 鼻を さすときは、「私」という 意味です。欧米で 胸をさすのと 同じです。

Japanese people point at their noses to refer to themselves. This is equivalent to the Western gesture of placing one's hand on the chest.

欧米（アメリカや ヨーロッパ）で 足を 組むのは いい マナーですが、日本では フォーマルなときに しては いけません。また、腕を 組むのは、日本では「考えている」という 意味に なります。

In Western countries (the United States and Europe), crossing one's legs is considered good manners. But in Japan, this is not acceptable on formal occasions. Also, crossing your arms indicates that you are thinking about something.

韓国の 立膝は いい マナーですが、日本では しては いけません。

In Korea, sitting with one knee raised is good manners. However, this is not true in Japan.

女性の 場合、足を 閉じるのが いい マナーです。

For women, closing the legs is considered proper etiquette.

「ください」「〜てください」

kudasai versus ~te kudasai

*https://matcha-jp.com/easy/7295

ラジープは 会社の 先輩と 居酒屋で お酒を 飲んでいます。先輩は 日本語を はやく 話すので、ラジープは よく わかりません。それで、ラジープは お願い しましたが……。

Rajeep is drinking at an *izakaya* bar with a senior colleague whose Japanese is too fast for Rajeep to understand. So Rajeep made a request, but...

"This beer is popular in Japan and…(talking fast)"
"Give me one more. "

"Umm…"

"One more?"

"Slowly please!"

"Slowly…?"

"…"

「ください」と「〜てください」

kudasai and *~te kudasai*

「ください」は、物が ほしいときに 使います。
なにかを お願いしたいとき、動詞の 「て形」を 使って 「〜てください」と 言わなければなりません。

The word *kudasai* is used when requesting an item or object. If you want someone to do an activity, you need to use the te-form of the verb before *kudasai*.

動詞　verbs	て形　te-form
見ます	見てください
行きます	行ってください
言います	言ってください
教えます	教えてください

また、「もういちど、おねがいします」か 「ゆっくり おねがいします」と 言っても いいです。

You can also say *mou ichido onegai shimasu* ("one more time, please") or *yukkuri onegai shimasu* ("slowly, please").

"Say that one more time slowly, please."

"Oh, sorry."

居酒屋　Izakaya

居酒屋は 日本の bar です。飲み物だけではなく、いろいろな 料理も あります。

An izakaya is a Japanese bar. It offers various food as well as drinks.

チェーンの居酒屋　Chain bars

値段が やすいです。初めての 人や 外国人、一人で 飲みたい 人には 入りやすいです。

Prices are reasonable at chain bars. They are good for first-timers, foreigners, and people who wish to drink alone.

子ども用の イスや、お皿、スプーンが あるので、家族で 楽しむことも できます。大きい チェーン店は 禁煙なので、安心です。

They offer chairs and cutlery for children, so all family members can enjoy a meal. Big chain stores are non-smoking, so you don't have to worry about that.

広い テーブルや、座敷(たたみの へや)が あるので、大学生や 会社の 飲み会にも よく 使います。

There are wide tables and *zashiki* (tatami rooms) for parties. College students and coworkers often use them for drinking parties.

赤ちょうちん、縄のれん *Akachouchin* and *nawanoren*

伝統的で 小さい 居酒屋は、サラリーマン（会社員）に 人気が あります。しかし、最近は 少なく なりました。

Smaller traditional bars are popular among "salarymen" (salaried company employees). However, the number of these bars has decreased in recent years.

赤い 提灯が 店の 前に あるので、「赤ちょうちん」と 言います。

Akachouchin are a type of bar that gets their name from the red lanterns hanging outside the storefront.

縄で 作った のれんが ある店は、「縄のれん」と 言います。

Nawanoren have a curtain made of ropes (*nawa*) at their entrance.

料理が 家庭的です。ときどき 地元の 料理も あります。また、オーナーと 会話を 楽しめます。

These establishments offer homemade food that sometimes includes local cuisine. Since they are small, patrons can even enjoy conversations with their owners.

東京新宿 のゴールデン街

＊https://matcha-jp.com/jp/3991

浅草ホッピー通り

＊https://matcha-jp.com/jp/63

屋台の 居酒屋も あります。とくに、おでんが 人気です。

There are also *yatai* or "food-stand" bars. Ones that specialize in oden are quite popular.

このような 店は、ときどき 料理の 値段が 書いて ありません。「いくらですか？」と 聞いてください。料理と お酒が 高い 場合も あります。

Yatai bars sometimes don't list the prices of their dishes. Since their food and drinks can be expensive, be sure to ask *ikura desu ka?* ("how much is it?").

コンセプト居酒屋　Concept izakaya

最近は、コンセプト居酒屋という、テーマが ある 居酒屋が 人気です。

Recently, bars with unique themes have become popular. These are called "concept izakaya."

● 学校居酒屋　School izakaya

教室のような 居酒屋です。メニューも 給食（学校の ごはん）です。

The interior of these bars looks like a classroom. The menu features items commonly served for school lunch in Japan.

● お化け居酒屋　Ghost izakaya

店の人は 日本の お化けの 服を 着ています。部屋の 中には、こわいものが たくさん あります。

Staff members in these bars wear Japanese ghost costumes. The rooms are filled with many scary props and decorations.

● 鉄道居酒屋　Railroad izakaya

店は 電車の 中のようです。そして、店の人も 駅員 みたいです。

The inside of these bars looks like the interior of a train. Their staff members also dress like station workers.

メニューには、電車の かたちの ごはんが あります。

Some of them even offer train-shaped rice on their menus.

● 居酒屋の料理の順番　Typical order of an izakaya meal

いくつかの店では、「お通し」という料理が最初にあります。

At some locations, an appetizer known as *o-tōshi* is served first.

「お通し」は小さな料理で、注文しなくても、店の人は持ってきます。たいてい300円〜500円くらいです。「お通し」を食べたくないときは、店の人に「お通しなしにできますか？」と聞いてください。

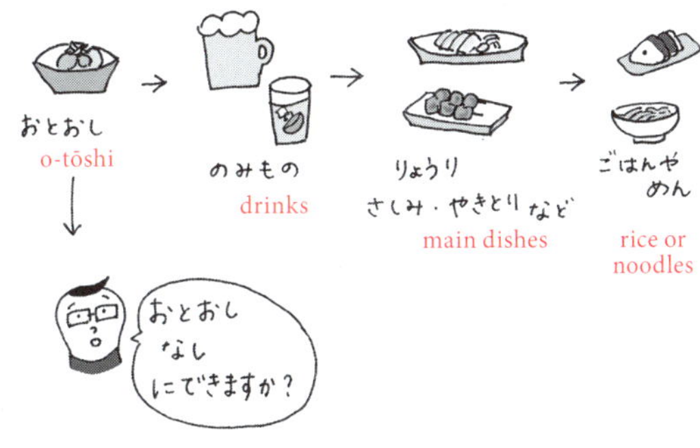

O-tōshi are small appetizers that are served even if you don't order them. They usually cost around ¥300 to ¥500. If you don't want any *o-tōshi*, ask the izakaya staff: *otōshi nashi ni dekimasu ka* ("Can I go without *otōshi*?").

人気の店に行くときは予約をしたほうがいいです。予約をキャンセルしたいときは「キャンセルしたいです。すみません」と言います。キャンセル料について、聞いたほうがいいです。

If you want to try a popular izakaya, you should make a reservation. When canceling a reservation, say: *Kyanseru shitai desu. Sumimasen.* You should also ask about any cancellation fee that might be charged.

有名な店や伝統的な店の場合、予約ができないことがあります。常連（いつも来る客）だけが店に入ることができます。そのような店には「一見さんお断り」という紙が、店の前にあります。入りたいときは、常連の人に紹介してもらいます。

With very famous or traditional restaurants, you can't make a reservation. Only regular customers can go in. These establishments will post a notice stating "*Ichigen-san o-ko-towari*" on the front door. To enter them, you need to have a regular patron to introduce you.

えいごのことば
English Words

*https://matcha-jp.com/easy/8081

クリスティーヌは、毎日、日本語を 勉 強 して、たくさんの ことばを 覚え ました。覚えた ことばで、店の人と 話しましたが……。

Christine studies Japanese every day and has learned many words. She tries to use them at shops, but...

"Do you have a haiiro no kaban?"
"A gray bag, right?"

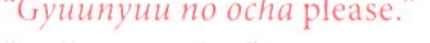

"Gyuunyuu no ocha please."
"Milk tea, right?"

"Is my Japanese wrong?"

えいごのことば
English words

日本語には、英語の ことばが たくさん あります。英語の ことばには 2種類あります。

Japanese people use a lot of English words! There are two types of words derived from English.

英語だけ使う Only English is used

食べ物や 飲み物など 日本に なかったものは 英語で 言うことが 多いです。

English is often used for things like food and drink items that did not originally exist in Japan.

英語で 言う (Say in English)	使わない ことば (Not used)
ミルクティー　milk tea	牛乳の お茶
ブラックコーヒー　black coffee	黒い コーヒー

日本語も英語も使う Both Japanese and English are used

下の ことばは 日本語と 英語 どちらでも いいです。でも、今は 英語を 使う 人が 多いです。

The words below can be used in either English or Japanese. Lately, though, many people use the English versions.

英語	日本語
グレーの バッグ　gray bag	灰色の カバン
リビング　living リビングルーム　living room	居間

"One milk tea, please."

"Okay."

外来語　*Gairaigo* (Loan words)

外国から　来た　ことばを　外来語と　言います。英語だけではなく、ポルトガル語、オランダ語、ドイツ語、フランス語などが　あります。昔、中国から　来た　ことばは　外来語と　言いません。

Words imported from other languages are called *gairaigo*. These include not only words from English but also Portuguese, Dutch, German, and French. Chinese words that entered the Japanese language long ago are not considered *gairaigo*.

食べ物　Food

パン　bread
ポルトガル語
Portuguese

コロッケ　croquette
フランス語
French

ステーキ　steak
英語
English

イクラ　red caviar
ロシア語
Russian

医療　Medical

ドイツ語と　オランダ語は　医療の　ことばに　使われています。

German and Dutch words are used for medical terms.

ドイツ語 German　：　アレルギー allergy　　ノイローゼ nervous breakdown

オランダ語 Dutch　：　メス scalpel　　ギプス cast

家の中　At home

ほとんどの　ことばが　英語です。

Most words for items found in homes are English.

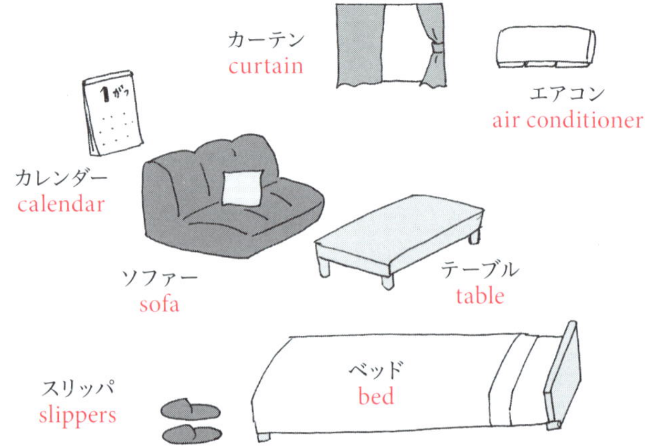

服 Clothes

ほとんどの ことばが 英語（えいご）ですが、ときどき 使（つか）いかたが 違（ちが）います。
Most clothing words are from English, although some of them are used differently.

街の中 In town

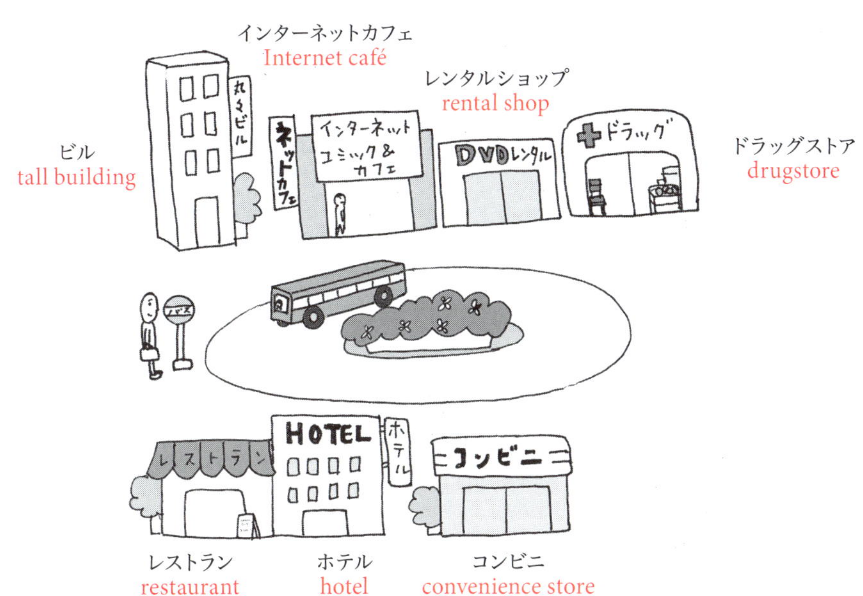

日本語の 動詞を 英語に して 使うことも あります。
Some verbs are derived directly from their English counterparts.

交流 する → コミュニケーションする
to communicate

支援する → サポートする
to support

挑戦する→チャレンジする
to challenge (oneself)

確認する→チェックする
to check

Q. どうして 日本語が あるのに 外来語を 使うの？
Why do Japanese people use gairaigo even though there are native words already?

A1. 日本人は、日本語は 古く、外来語は 新しく 感じます。
Japanese people feel like Japanese words are old, but gairaigo sounds new and exciting.

A2. 日本語は 伝統的で、外来語は おしゃれな 感じが します。
Japanese words sound traditional, while gairaigo sounds modern and stylish.

An example conversation between young Japanese people

A: クリスマス どうする？　What are we gonna do for Christmas?

B: クリスマスライブ 行かない？　Let's go to a live Christmas show

A: どの バンド？　Which band?

B: いろんな バンド。Eチケットだから スマホで とれるよ。
There are a bunch of bands. It's electronic tickets, so we can get them on our smart-phones.

A: でも クリスマスは バイトの シフト 入ってる。
But I have my part-time job on Christmas day.

B: どこで バイトしてるの？　Where are you working?

A: カフェ。スイーツが おいしいよ。　At a café. Their sweets are good.

B: キッチン？　ホール？　Kitchen or dining?

A: ホールだよ。ウェイトレス。　Dining. I'm a waitress.

B: オーナー やさしい？　Is the owner nice?

A: うん、スタッフ みんな やさしいよ。それに メイク 自由だし、エプロン もらえるし。
Yeah, all the staff are nice to me. Also, I can wear makeup and they give me an apron for free.

B: いいね。おれは ウェブデザインの バイトしてるよ。イラストとか ロゴ 作ってるんだ。
That's good. I'm doing web design part-time. Making illustrations and logos.

A: かっこいい〜。　Cool!

Q：お寺と 神社の 違いは なんですか？

What is the difference between temples and shrines?

A：

神社 **Shrines**

神社は 神道のものです。神道は 大昔から ある 宗教 です。神道の 神様は たくさん いて、八百万の 神と 言われています。たいていは 自然 (山、木、岩など) が神様です。神様の ための お祭りが あります。

Shrines are a part of Shinto, a set of religious beliefs from long ago. Shinto has many gods, which are collectively referred to as *yaoyorozu no kami* ("eight million gods"). Most of these are based on features of the natural world, such as mountains, trees, and rocks. Festivals for the Shinto gods are held throughout Japan.

また、天皇は、神話の 中の 神様の 子孫だ と 言われています。

Emperors of Japan are also said to be descendants of a Shinto goddess found in myths.

お正月や 特別な 日に 神社に 行って お祈りをします。また 結婚式を する人も います。

On New Year's Day and other special occasions, people visit shrines to pray. Some people also choose to have their wedding ceremonies at Shinto shrines.

参道の 真ん中は 神様が 歩く ところですから、歩かないほうが いいです。

The center of the street that approaches a shrine is for gods to use, so it's best not to walk right down the middle.

神社の 中に ある 岩や 木に 登らないでください。神聖な ものです。

Don't climb the rocks and trees you see in shrines—they are sacred.

お参りの仕方　How to pray at a shrine

お金を 賽銭箱という 箱に 入れます。いくらでも いいです。

Put money into the *saisenbako* (offering box). Any amount is fine.

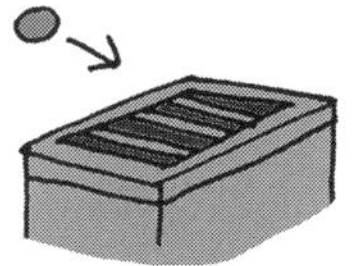

次に、鐘を ならします。

Next, ring the bell.

それから、2回 お辞儀を して、2回 手を たたきます。最後に また1回 お辞儀を します。

Bow twice, clap your hands twice, then bow once more.

＊神社によって ちがいます。大切なことは お辞儀を して 神様を 尊敬する ことですから 順 番や 数を 心配しないで ください。

The exact procedure depends on the shrine. But the important thing is to bow and show respect to the *kamisama* (Japanese deities), so don't worry about getting the order or number of motions correct.

お寺は、仏教の たてものです。仏教は 600年ごろ、中国から 来ました。悟りを 開く 目的ですが、普通の 人は 安心の ために 仏像（仏陀の 像）に お祈りを しました。江戸時代に 政府は すべての 人が どこかの お寺に 入らないといけない と決めて、お寺で 葬式を するようになりました。

Temples are based on Buddhism, which was imported from China around 600 B.C. Although the ultimate purpose of Buddhism is enlightenment, most people pray to Buddha statues for a sense of relief. In the Edo period, the Japanese government mandated that all people must belong to a temple. Funerals were then also held at temples.

今も 葬式や お盆には お坊さんが 死んだ 人の ために お経を 唱えます。

Even now, monks chant sutra for the deceased at funerals and during the *obon* holiday.

神道と 仏教は 衝突するのではなく、融合したので、神社と お寺が 一緒に なって いる ところが いくつか あります。

Shinto incorporated Buddhism rather than clashing with it, which led to some places mixing the two belief systems.

いま、ほとんどの 日本人は とくに 宗教 が ない と 言います。日本人にとって、神道と 仏教は、生活の 一部のような ものです。

Nowadays, most Japanese people state that they don't subscribe to a religion. For them, Shinto and Buddhism are just a part of their life.

こんなときどうする？

What to do when…?

ラジープは、毎日、一緒に働いている人に「おはようございます。元気ですか？」とあいさつをします。しかし、なにか変です。

Rajeep says "Good morning, how are you?" to his co-workers every morning. But there seems to be something wrong with that.

[Monday]
"Good morning. How are you?"
"Good morning. I'm good."

[Tuesday]
"Good morning. How are you?"
"Good morning. I'm good. Why?"

"Good morning. It's hot..." "Hmm..."
"Good morning. Yeah, it's hot today."
"Good morning. How..."

日々のあいさつ
Everyday greetings

毎日 会う 人に あまり 「元気ですか」 とは 言いません。

「おはようございます」「こんにちは」「こんばんは」だけで だいじょうぶです。

また、日本人は 「いい 天気ですね」 や 「暑いですね」 など 天気について よく 話します。

Japanese people don't say "How are you?" to people they meet every day. It's okay to just say things like "Good morning," "Hello," or "Good evening." Conversational topics such as the weather are also often used when greeting someone ("Nice weather, isn't it?" or "It's a hot one!", for example).

ひさしぶりに 会ったときや、病気の 後に 「元気ですか」 と 言います。

また、いつもと 違う 顔のとき (例えば 悲しそうだったり、大変そうだったりした とき) も 「元気ですか」 と 言います。

Use *genki desu ka* when it has been a long time since you've seen the person, or after they have been sick. You can also say it when someone looks different (sad, troubled, etc.).

"Good morning. It's nice weather, isn't it?"

"Good morning.
Yes, the weather is nice."

<ruby>他<rt>ほか</rt></ruby>のあいさつ　Other greetings

<ruby>会社<rt>かいしゃ</rt></ruby>で　At the office

<ruby>仕事<rt>しごと</rt></ruby>を している <ruby>間<rt>あいだ</rt></ruby>に、<ruby>同僚<rt>どうりょう</rt></ruby>に <ruby>会<rt>あ</rt></ruby>ったときは「おつかれさまです」と <ruby>言<rt>い</rt></ruby>います。

<ruby>仕事<rt>しごと</rt></ruby>が <ruby>終<rt>お</rt></ruby>わって、<ruby>同僚<rt>どうりょう</rt></ruby>より <ruby>早<rt>はや</rt></ruby>く <ruby>帰<rt>かえ</rt></ruby>るときは「お<ruby>先<rt>さき</rt></ruby>に <ruby>失礼<rt>しつれい</rt></ruby>します」と <ruby>言<rt>い</rt></ruby>います。

そして、「おつかれさまでした」と <ruby>答<rt>こた</rt></ruby>えます。

When you see your coworkers during work hours, you can say *otsukaresama desu*.

If you leave work earlier than your coworkers, say *osaki ni shitsurei shimasu*.

They will say *otsukaresama deshita* in response.

<ruby>友達<rt>ともだち</rt></ruby>と　With your friends

<ruby>会<rt>あ</rt></ruby>ったとき　Upon meeting　　　　<ruby>別<rt>わか</rt></ruby>れるとき　When saying goodbye

<ruby>近所<rt>きんじょ</rt></ruby>の<ruby>人<rt>ひと</rt></ruby>に<ruby>会<rt>あ</rt></ruby>ったとき　When seeing a neighbor

ひさしぶりに会ったとき

フォーマル　formal

カジュアル　casual

季節ごとのあいさつ
Seasonal greetings and topics

春 Spring
はる

あったかく なりましたね。
It's gotten warm.

桜　cherry blossom
さくら

夏 Summer
なつ

今日も 暑いですね。
きょう　あつ
Today is hot, too.

夏祭り　summer festival
なつまつ

秋 Fall
あき

すずしく なりましたね。
It's gotten cooler.

紅葉　autumn leaves
こうよう

冬 Winter
ふゆ

寒いですね。
さむ
It's cold, isn't it?

雪まつり　snow festival
ゆき
クリスマス　Christmas

ホテルや 旅館の 人に 挨拶するときは、「こんにちは」だけでも だいじょうぶです。でも、ホームステイや 民宿＊で 長く 泊まるときは、「お世話に なります」と 言ったほうが いいでしょう。帰るときには「お世話に なりました」と 言います。

When greeting the staff of a hotel or ryokan, you can say just *konnichiwa*. However, if you will be staying for an extended period of time at a *minshuku*＊ or private Japanese residence, you should say *osewani narimasu*. When leaving, use the past tense (*osewani narimashita*).

泊まっている 間に 出かけるときは「いってきます」、帰ってきたときは「ただいま」と 言います。

When you go out during your stay, say *itte kimasu*; when returning, say *tadaima*.

＊民宿：家族で 経営しています。ちいさくて、伝統的な 部屋が 多いです。
　　Minshuku are family owned and operated. Their rooms are often small and traditional.

旅館は 民宿よりも 大きくて 高いです。伝統的です。他にも、ペンション、Airbnb、宿坊など いろいろ あります。

Ryokan are larger and more expensive than minshuku, but they are also traditional. Aside from these, there are *penshon* (boarding houses), Airbnbs, and *shukubou*.

宿坊について *Shukubou*

最近、お寺の 中に 泊まるのが 人気です。お寺での 体験が できます。しかし、それは 普通の ホテルや 旅行者のための アクティビティではありません。修行を 体験する ところです。

Recently, staying at a lodging facility inside a temple has become popular. Such guests can experience the activities that go on in the temple. However, this is not a normal hotel or tourist activity. It is the experience of training as a monk.

大きな 声で 話すのは よく ありません。また、お寺の 物に さわったり、落書きを しては いけません。神社も 同じ マナーが あります。

You can't speak in loud voices, touch the temple's holy objects, or write graffiti. These same manners are also required when visiting shrines.

「いらっしゃいませ」
Welcome

＊https://matcha-jp.com/easy/7446

インドネシアから 来<ruby>き</ruby>た スリは、はじめて 日本<ruby>にほん</ruby>の スーパーへ 行<ruby>い</ruby>きました。店<ruby>みせ</ruby>の人<ruby>ひと</ruby>が 「いらっしゃいませ」 を たくさん 言<ruby>い</ruby>うので、スリは、すこし びっくりしました。

Suri is from Indonesia. She has gone to a Japanese supermarket for the first time. At the store, the employees say *irasshaimase* a lot, so she is a little puzzled.

"Welcome! (irasshaimase!)"

"Hello…"　"Hello…"

"Welcome! Try this!"

"Welcome!"
"Welcome!"　"Welcome!"

"Hello"　"Hello"
"Hello"

お店でのあいさつ
Greetings at the store

「いらっしゃいませ」は、店の人が お客さんに 言う 挨拶です。店の人が 「いらっしゃいませ」と 言うとき、返事を しなくても だいじょうぶです。
小さい お店では 「こんにちは」や 「こんばんは」と 言っても いいですよ。
また、下の 絵のように、にっこりするのも いいと 思います。

Irasshaimase is a greeting to customers. You don't need to answer every time a store employee says it.

If it is a small shop, you could say *konnichiwa* or *konbanwa*.

You can also just smile in response, as in the picture below.

日本のスーパー　Japanese Supermarkets

スーパーで、日本らしい 野菜や 生きている 魚を 刺し身にして 買うことも できます。

At supermarkets, you can buy typical Japanese vegetables and sashimi made from live fish.

お米が たくさん ありますが、ぜんぶ ジャポニカ米 という 種類です。ジャスミンライスや バスマティライスは 普通の スーパーには ありません。

They have many types of rice, although all are of the Japonica variety. Normal supermarkets don't have rices like jasmine or basmati.

日本では カートに 直接 品物を 入れません。かごを カートの 中に 入れてください。子どもを 乗せる 車の カートも あります。

In Japan, you can't put items directly into the cart. Put a basket in the cart, then put your items inside it. There are even carts styled after cars for children to ride in.

レジの人は 空のかごに 品物を 入れます。
The cashier will transfer your items into an empty basket.

自分で 袋に 入れますが、エコバッグ(マイバッグ)を レジの人に 渡すだけでも だいじょうぶです。
You can then put your items into your reusable shopping bag (*mai baggu*) or just hand your bag to the cashier.

ほとんどの 店には ポイントカードが あります。たいてい、ポイントは お金と同じように 使えます。カードが ほしかったら、「カードを 作りたいです」と 言います。
Most stores have point cards. You can usually use accumulated points instead of money to pay for items. If you would like a card, say *kādo o tsukuritai desu*.

VISAなどの クレジットカードを 使うとき、店の人は 「一括で よろしいですか」と 聞きます。もし 「はい」と 答えたら、普通に 1回で 全部 払います。日本の クレジットカードは 何回かに 分けて 払えるからです。
When paying with a credit card such as Visa, the cashier will ask *ikkatsu de yoroshii desu ka*? If you answer *Hai*, your total will be paid all at once as normal. However, Japanese credit cards also offer the option to split the total amount up over several payments.

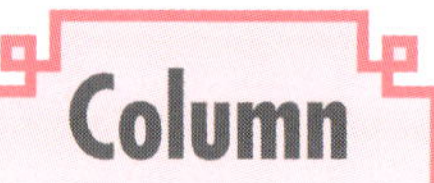

日本人がよく行く店　Popular stores in Japan

コンビニ　Convenience Stores

すぐに 食べられる おいしいものが たくさんあります。
Convenience stores offer immediate access to many tasty items.

- ファミリーマート、セブンイレブン、ローソンなど
  Family Mart, 7-Eleven, Lawson, etc.

This is different from what we have in China, but it's still good.

ドラッグストア　Drugstores

薬だけではなく、日用品（毎日 使う 物）や お菓子などが 安いので おすすめです。

Drugstores aren't just for medicine—they also offer daily necessities, snacks, and other items at reasonable prices.

- ウェルシア、マツモトキヨシ、サンドラッグなど
  Welcia, Matsumotokiyoshi, Sundrug, etc.

ディスカウントストア・100円ショップ　Discount Stores / ¥100 Shops

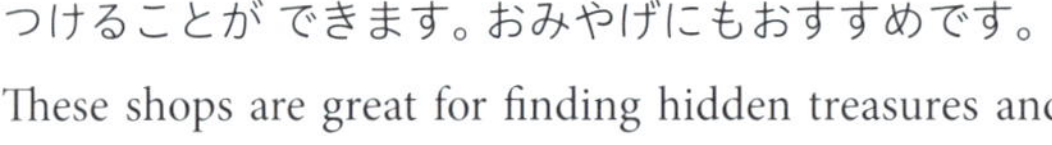

宝 探しのように、おもしろいもの、便利で 安い物を 見つけることが できます。おみやげにもおすすめです。

These shops are great for finding hidden treasures and deals on interesting items and souvenirs.

- ドン・キホーテ、オリンピック、ダイソー、Seria など
  Don Quixote, Olympic, Daiso, Seria, etc.

雑貨店　Variety Shops

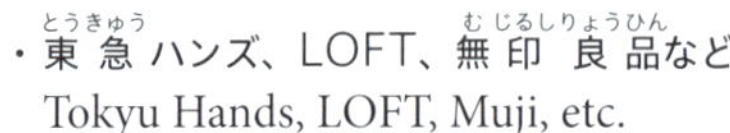

かわいい 文房具や おしゃれな 小物が あって、見るだけでも 楽しめます。

Variety shops have lots of cute stationery and stylish accessories, which makes them a good choice for window-shopping.

- 東急 ハンズ、LOFT、無印 良品など
  Tokyu Hands, LOFT, Muji, etc.

大型電器店　Appliance Stores

免税で 買い物も できるし、外国語が 話せる スタッフも いるので、外国人に とても 人気です。

These are quite popular with foreigners because they often have duty-free products as well as staff who are fluent in other languages.

・ヨドバシカメラ、ヤマダ電機、ビックカメラ、ラオックスなど
　Yodobashi Camera, Yamada Denki, Bic Camera, Laox, etc.

ホームセンター・リサイクルショップ・家具店
Home Centers, Recycle Shops, and Furniture Stores

日本に 住んでいる 人に おすすめです。大きいものは 配達も してくれます。

These are recommended for people living in Japan. They will even deliver bulky items to you.

・ニトリ、コーナン、トレジャーファクトリーなど
　Nitori, Kohnan, Treasure Factory, etc.

ショッピングモール　Shopping Malls

若い人、家族に おすすめです。映画館、フードコートなどが あり、一日 楽しめます。

Shopping malls are recommended for young people and families. They have amenities such as movie theaters and food courts that make for a fun day of shopping.

・ららぽーと、イオンモール、東京 スカイツリータウンなど
　Lalaport, AEON Mall, Tokyo Sky Tree Town, etc.

デパート　Department Stores

高級な ギフトや、フォーマルな 服を 買いたい 人に おすすめです。地下には、見た目が 美しい 食べ物が あるので ギフトに 人気です。

If you want to buy formal attire or luxury items, department stores are your best bet. Their underground levels are popular for delicious and visually spectacular products that make great gifts.

・伊勢丹、西武、三越など
　Isetan, Seibu, Mitsukoshi, etc.

特急の乗りかた
Riding the express train

＊https://matcha-jp.com/easy/7656

林が 電車を 待っていると、特急 電車が 来ました。特急 電車の 次は、いつも 林が 乗っている 普通電車が 来ます。どちらの 電車も 同じ 駅に 行くので、林は 早く 来た「特急 電車」に 乗りました。

While Rin was waiting on the platform, a limited express train came. The next train would be the local train he normally takes. But since both trains go to the same station, he takes the limited express.

"Limited express…
This will be faster."

"Fast!
Clean!"

"Show me your limited express ticket, please."
"Ah?"

"You cannot use this."
"This is no good?"

いろいろな電車の種類
Various train types

電車には、特急、急行、快速、普通など、いろいろな 種類が あります。特急や 急行などは、普通の 料金 以外に、料金が 必要かもしれません。心配な ときは、駅員さんに、切符が ただしいか どうか 聞いたほうが いいでしょう。

There are various types of Japanese trains: express, rapid, local etc. Trains like the limited express and express might cost more than a standard ticket. If you aren't sure which you should take, ask a station employee.

日本語	英語
特急	limited express train
急行	express train
快速	rapid train
準急	semi-express train
普通	local train

"Is this ticket good for this train?"

"You will also need a limited express ticket."

鉄道の種類　Types of railway

JR Japanese Railway	日本中に あります。新幹線はJR です。外国人旅行者には JR rail pass が あります。 There are JR lines all over Japan. The shinkansen is also owned by JR. The JR Rail Pass is available for foreign travelers. *https://japanrailpass.net/en/　*https://matcha-jp.com/jp/672
私鉄 Private railway	それぞれの 都市には 私鉄が あります。JR rail passは 使えません。 Every sizable city has private rail lines. JR Rail Passes can't be used on these railways.
地下鉄 Subway	東京、名古屋、大阪など 大きな 都市に あります。安くて 安全で 便利です。 Some major cities such as Tokyo, Nagoya, and Osaka have subways. They are inexpensive, safe, and convenient for getting around.

田舎には、かわいくて、すてきな 電車が あります。

In the countryside, there are many cute and lovely trains.

わたらせ渓谷鉄道
Watarase Keikokutetsudo

真岡鉄道
Moka Tetsudo

JR 氷見線　JR Himi Line

海の すぐ 隣を 走ります。とくに 雨晴駅は 有名です。その駅の 名前は「雨が 晴れる」という 意味だからです。

This train runs along the coastline. Amaharashi Station is especially famous. The station gets its name from the phrase *ame ga hareru*, which means "rain clears up."

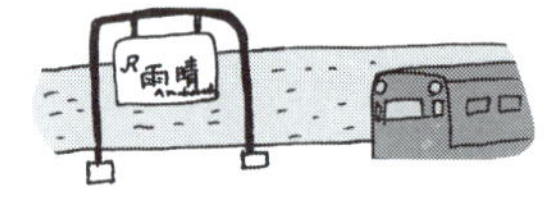

会津鉄道　Aizu Tetsudo

昔の 日本の 雰囲気が 楽しめます。
芦ノ牧温泉駅には、ねこ駅長が います。

You can enjoy the Japan of the past on this railway. Ashinomakionsen Station has a cat for a station master.

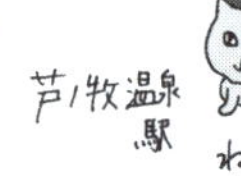

新幹線 Shinkansen (bullet train)

遠くに 行くときは、新幹線が 速くて 便利です。

When traveling to distant locations, the shinkansen is very fast and convenient.

東海道・山陽新幹線　　東京 ⇔ 名古屋、京都、新大阪、博多

Tokaido / Sanyo Shinkansen　Tokyo ⇔ Nagoya / Kyoto / Shin-Osaka / Hakata

東海道・山陽新幹線には 3種類の 新幹線が あって、速さと 値段も 違います。予約には Smart EX という サイトが 便利です。

There are three types of Tokaido / Sanyo Shinkansen, and they differ in both speed and price. The Smart EX website is useful for making shinkansen reservations.

＊https://smart-ex.jp/en/index.php

のぞみ：大きな 駅だけ 止まるので、一番 速いです。東京から 新大阪まで 2時間半ぐらいです。

Nozomi is the fastest because it only stops at the largest stations. It travels from Tokyo to Shin-Osaka in about 2.5 hours.

ひかり：2番目に 速いです。東京から 新大阪まで 3時間ぐらい かかります。

Hikari is the second fastest, making the journey from Tokyo to Shin-Osaka in 3 hours.

こだま：全部の 駅に 止まります。東京から 新大阪まで 4時間ぐらい かかります。

Kodama stops at all stations, so it requires about 4 hours to go from Tokyo to Shin-Osaka.

北陸新幹線 あさま　　　　東京 ⇔ 長野

Hokuriku Shinkansen Asama　　Tokyo ⇔ Nagano

東北・秋田新幹線 こまち　　東京 ⇔ 秋田

Tohoku / Akita Shinkansen Komachi　　Tokyo ⇔ Akita

この他にも、もっと 種類が あります。There are even more types than these.

路線図　**Rail Transit Map**

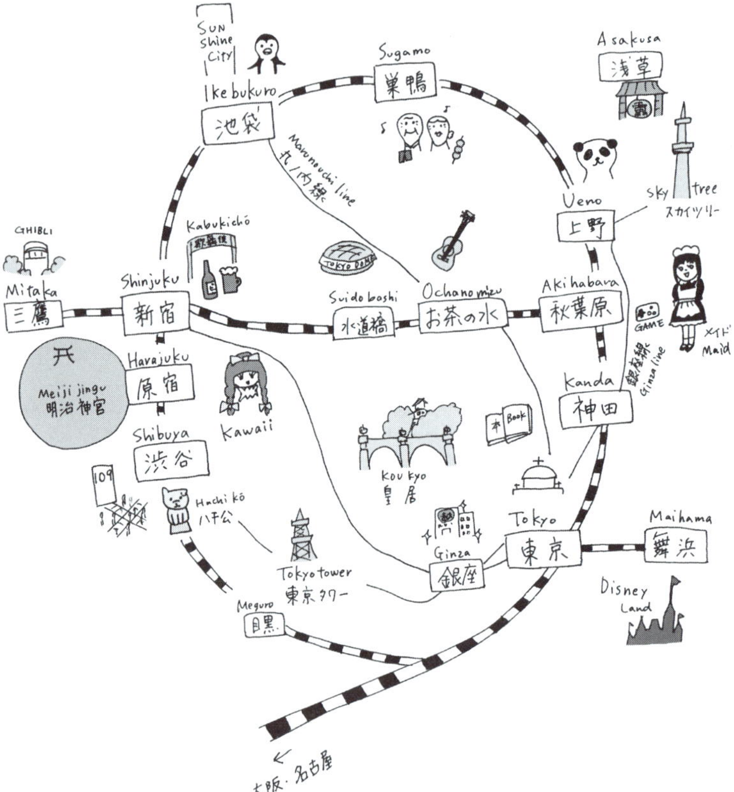

にんき　　ばしょ
人気の 場所は、ほとんど JRの 山手線と 中央線で 行くことが できます。路線図の 白と黒の線が JRです。丸の内線と 銀座線は 地下鉄 (東京メトロ) です。この他にも、たくさんの 地下鉄が あります。

You can reach almost any popular destination via the JR Yamanote and Chuo Lines. JR is represented by a black and white dotted line on railway maps. The Marunouchi and Ginza Lines are part of the subway (Tokyo Metro). There are many more trains in addition to these.

＊ https://matcha-jp.com/jp/list/?region=41

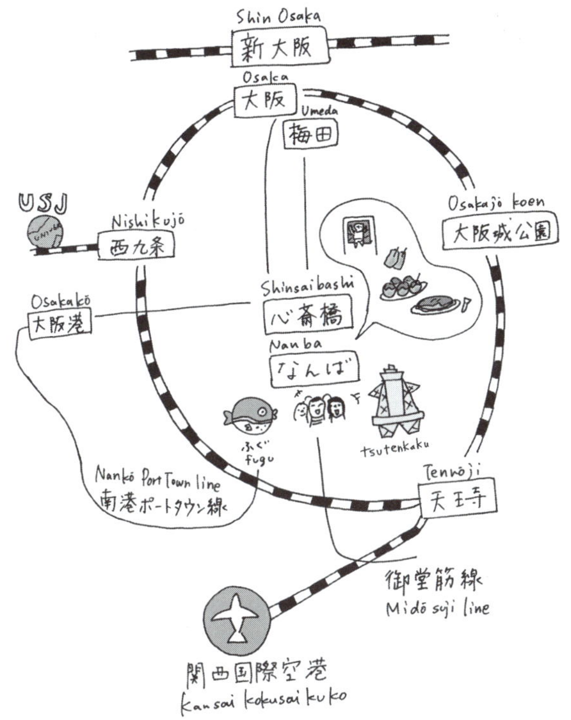

おおさか かんじょうせん ちかてつみどうすじせん にんき ばしょ い とく しんさいばし
大阪は JR 環状線と 地下鉄御堂筋線で 人気の 場所に 行けます。特に 「心斎橋」と 「な
あいだ どうとんぼり かわ そ みせ
んば」の 間にある 「道頓堀」という ところは、川に 沿って たくさん レストランや 店が
たの
あって 楽しいです。

In Osaka, the JR Kanjo Line and the Midosuji Metro Line can take you to popular spots.
In particular, a fun area between Shinsaibashi and Nanba known as Dōtonbori is packed
with restaurants and other shops along the river.

み どうすじせん どうぶつえんえき ちか どく さかな た みせ
御堂筋線の 「動物園駅」の 近くに、「ふぐ」という 毒の ある 魚が 食べられる 店が あり
しんがた へいてん
ましたが、新型コロナウイルスのせいで 閉店して しまいました。

There was a famous restaurant near Dōbutsuen Station on the Midōsuji Line where
you could try the poisonous fugu fish, but it was forced to close due to the coronavirus
pandemic.

＊ https://matcha-jp.com/jp/list/?region=33

「日本」の読みかた
How to read the word "Japan"

＊https://matcha-jp.com/easy/9256

クリスティーヌは テレビで 「にっぽん」 という 言葉を 見ました。
次の日 いけばなの レッスンで、クリスティーヌは 「にっぽんが 好き」と 山田さんに 言いました。それを 聞いて 山田さんは、すこし 混乱している ようです。

Christine saw the word *nippon* on TV. Then next day, she said *nippon ga suki* to Ms. Yamada, who was a little puzzled by that...

"Gan...ba...re...
NIPPON!"

[the next day]
"You really like ikebana don't you, Christine?"
"Yes!"

Japanese cuisine, Japanese tea, Japanese language,
Japanese people (keeps repeating *nippon*)

"Oh..."
"I love Nippon!"

日本の読みかた
Reading the word "Japan"

日本は「にほん」と「にっぽん」の 2つの 読みかたが あります。

「にほん」と「にっぽん」は どちらも 正しいですが、だいたいは「にほん」と 読みます。

There are two pronunciations for the word "Japan": *nihon* and *nippon*. While both are correct, it is usually pronounced *nihon*.

	にほん	にっぽん
日本	「にほん」 69%	「にっぽん」 31%
日本人	「にほんじん」 90%	「にっぽんじん」 10%
日本語	「にほんご」 97%	「にっぽんご」 3%
日本一	「にほんいち」 51%	「にっぽんいち」 49%
日本大使館	「にほんたいしかん」 88%	「にっぽんたいしかん」 12%

※20歳〜 81歳の 男の人と 女の人 ぜんぶで 51人に 読みかたを 聞きました。

* Fifty-one men and women between the ages of 20 and 81 were asked how they pronounce the words.

※テレビ朝日『「日本」の 読みは「にほん」？「にっぽん」？』から引用しました。

* Sourced from the TV Asahi website (https://www.tv-asahi.co.jp/announcer/nihongo/labo/lab_013/body.html).

「にほん」と 読む人が 多いですね。しかし、スポーツなどで 日本を 応援したり、「がんばろう」という 気持ちを 伝えるときには「にっぽん」と 言う 人が 多いようです。

Most people say *nihon*. But when rooting for Japan in sports or otherwise communicating your feelings, *nippon* is popular.

「日本」という呼びかた　Referring to *nihon*

むかしは、やまと や わこく といって、日本 という 名前では ありませんでした。
Long ago, Japan was known as *yamato or wakoku*—the name *nihon* did not exist.

600年ぐらいに、日本の 天皇は 中国に 手紙を 書きました。「日の出る ところから 日の没する ところへ」と 書いたので、中国の 王様が 怒った という 話が あります。
Around 600 AD, the emperor of Japan wrote a letter to China. In it, he wrote "from the land of the rising sun to the land of the setting sun," which angered the Chinese emperor.

日本は 中国の 東に ありますから、日の出る ところ という 意味でした。「日の出る」と 「日の本」は 同じような 意味ですから、「日の本」から 「日本」という 名前が できました。
He wrote that expression because Japan is located to the east of China. 日の出る and 日の本 both mean "the origin of the sun." Eventually, 日の本 became 日本, the word that is now used to refer to the country of Japan.

読みかたは、「ひのもと」から 「にっぽん」と 「にほん」に なりました。
The pronunciation changed from *hinomoto* (ひのもと) to *nippon* and *nihon*.

2009年に、政府は 「にっぽん」と 「にほん」の どちらでも いい と 決めました。
In 2009, the government decided that both *nippon* and *nihon* are acceptable pronunciations.

Japan という呼<ruby>呼<rt>よ</rt></ruby>びかた　Referring to Japan

1300年ごろ、マルコ・ポーロが 中国に 来ました。中国南部の「日本国」の 発音 ji-pen-quo を cipangu と思って、ヨーロッパに 伝えました。

Around the start of the thirteenth century, Marco Polo visited China. While there, he heard people in southern China refer to Japan as *ji-pen-guo*. To him, it sounded like "cipangu," so he taught that pronunciation upon his return to Europe.

Cipangu は、国によって Yappon や Giappone、Japon などに変わって、英語では Japan になりました。

The name Cipangu then became Yappon, Giappone, Japon, or something else depending on the language. In English, it became "Japan."

他の国の呼びかた（例）　Referring to other countries — Examples

アメリカ *Amerika*　United States	エジプト *Ejiputo*　Egypt	ケニア *Kenia*　Kenya	ドイツ *Doitsu*　Germany
イギリス *Igirisu*　United Kingdom	エチオピア *Echiopia*　Ethiopia	コロンビア *Koronbia*　Colombia	ナイジェリア *Naijeria*　Nigeria
イタリア *Itaria*　Italy	オーストラリア *Ōsutoraria*　Australia	スイス *Suisu*　Switzerland	ブラジル *Burajiru*　Brazil
インド *Indo*　India	オランダ *Oranda*　Holland	スペイン *Supein*　Spain	ベトナム *Betonamu*　Vietnam
インドネシア *Indoneshia*　Indonesia	カナダ *Kanada*　Canada	タイ *Tai*　Thailand	中国 *Chūgoku*　China
ウクライナ *Ukuraina*　Ukraine	ギリシャ *Girisha*　Greece	トルコ *Toruko*　Turkey	韓国 *Kankoku*　South Korea

人の呼びかた　Addressing people

日本では、「あなた」と 呼ぶのは 少し 失礼な 感じが します。名前を 呼びます。
名前が わからないときは 主語を 言いません。

In Japan, addressing someone as *anata* (you) is considered rude. Address people by their names instead.

If you don't know the person's name, just omit the subject entirely.

医者や 先生は 名前を 言わないで 「せんせい」 だけを よく 言います。

Doctors and teachers are usually addressed simply as *sensei* rather than by name.

バーの店主　Bar owners

男の人は 「マスター」、女の人は 「ママ」 と 呼びます。

Male bar owners are addressed as "master" (*masutā*), while female owners are called *mama*.

日本料理店の店主　Owners of Japanese restaurants

男 の人は 「ご主人」、女の人は 「おかみさん」 と 呼びます。

Men are referred to as *goshujin* and women as *okami-san*.

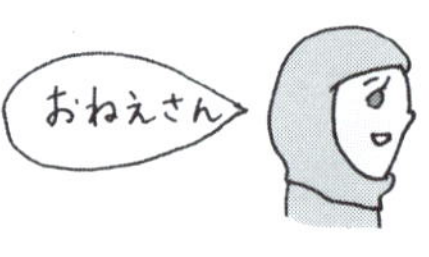

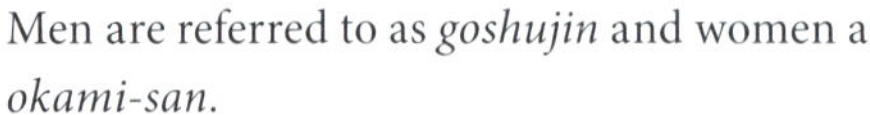

若い 店員を 「おねえさん」「おにいさん」 と 呼ぶことも ありますが、普通は 「すみません」 だけ言うことが 一番 多いです。

Young employees of a shop are sometimes referred to as *oneesan* (if they are female) or *oniisan* (if they are male), but most people just say *sumimasen*.

家族の呼びかた　Family members

大人は、他の人の 前で お父さんを「ちち」、お母さんを「はは」と 言います。

In front of other people, adults refer to their own mother as *haha* and their own father as *chichi*.

他の人の 両親を 呼ぶときは「ちち」「はは」を 使いません。「おとうさん」「おかあさん」と 言います。

When referring to someone else's parents, use *otōsan* and *okāsan* instead of *chichi* and *haha*.

日本の名前　Japanese names

日本では、家族の 名前を 最初に 言います。それは「みょうじ」と 言います。そして ふつうは みょうじを 呼びます。

In Japanese, last names (*myouji*) come first. Usually, we address and refer to people by their *myouji*.

高橋　　浩紀

みょうじ　　なまえ
last name　　first name

日本では 伝統的な スタイルは 上から 下です。上の 名前、下の 名前も 使います。

Traditionally, Japanese is written from top to bottom, so we also say *ue no namae* (upper name) and *shita no namae* (lower name).

高橋　上　ue

浩紀　下　shita

みそ汁の飲みかた
How to eat misoshiru

*https://matcha-jp.com/easy/9729

インドから来た ラジープは、ほとんど 毎日 カレーを 食べています。インドでは、手で カレーを 食べますが、日本では スプーンを 使って ごはんに かけて食べます。それで ラジープは、みそ汁も スプーンで ごはんに かけて 食べる と 思いました。

Rajeep is from India, and he eats curry almost every day. In India, he eats curry with his hands. But in Japan, curry is poured over rice and eaten with a spoon. Rajeep thinks miso soup is eaten that same way.

"This is the first time we've eaten traditional Japanese food together."

"Yes, it is." "Oh, this is not curry!"

"Miso soup, right?"

"Yeah, but…"

"Don't use a spoon!!"

"How do you eat it?"

みそ汁の飲みかた
How to eat misoshiru

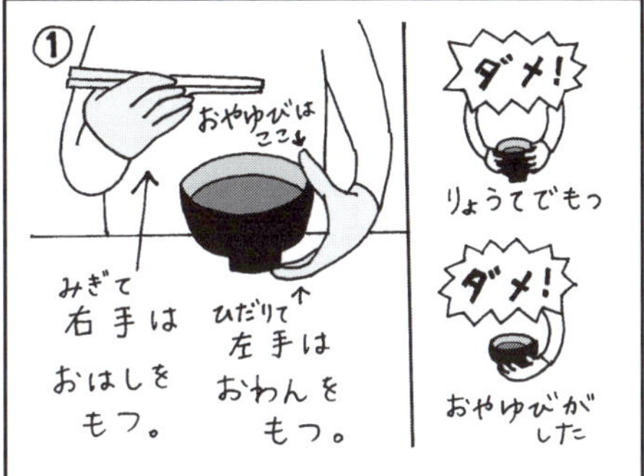

Bad!

Holding the bowl with both hands.

Bad!

Placing your thumbs under the bowl.

Hold your chopsticks with your right hand and the bowl with your left hand, placing your thumb on top of the bowl.

Bad!

Don't point your chopsticks away from the bowl and toward other people.

Put your chopsticks in the bowl and use them to hold the ingredients in place while you drink.

和食 Washoku (Japanese cuisine)

和食 というと 寿司が 有名ですが、家で 毎日 食べる 食事は、「主食」の ごはんと みそ汁、そして 「おかず」 です。

When it comes to washoku, sushi is the most famous dish. But at home, typical meals include the staple foods (*shushoku*) of rice and miso soup combined with other dishes (*okazu*).

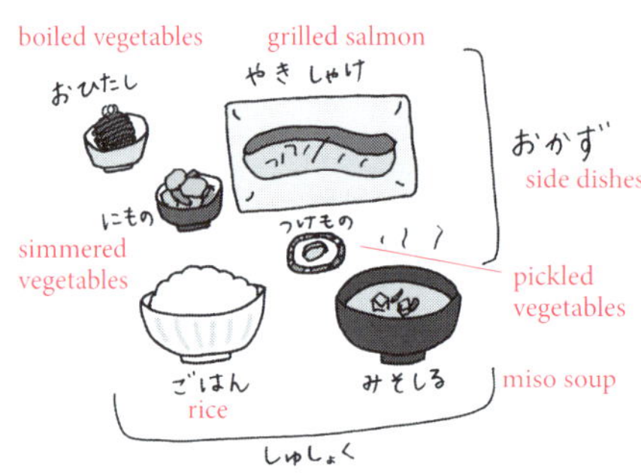

ふつうは 白いごはんですが、五目ご はん、栗ごはん、わかめごはん など も あります。

Normally rice is just white rice, but there are more: five-ingredient rice, chestnut rice, wakame seaweed rice.

みそ汁も いつも ちがう 材料 で 作ります。たいていは 野菜、わかめ、豆腐です。みそ の 代わりに しょう油を 使うことも あります。お吸い物と 言います。

Miso soup is made with many different ingredients. Generally, it includes vegetables, wakame (seaweed), and tofu. Sometimes, soy sauce is used instead of miso, in which case it is referred to as *o-suimono*.

伝統的な おかずは 焼き魚です。
それから 野菜 や 海草も よく 食べます。

Traditional okazu is grilled fish.
Vegetables and seaweed are also eaten often.

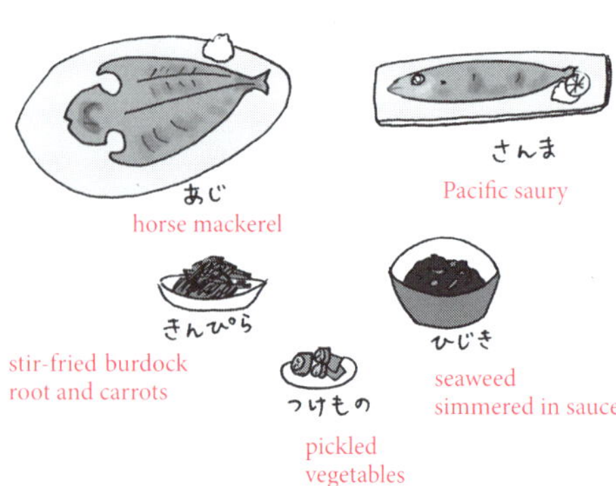

和食の歴史　History of Japanese cuisine

1　ごはん、しる、魚や貝、野菜の 食事で、肉は ほとんど 食べませんでした。
Meals consisted of rice, soup, fish and shellfish, and vegetables. Meat was rarely eaten.

2　すしと そばが できました。天ぷらが ポルトガルから 来ました。
Sushi and soba were invented. Tempura arrived from Portugal.

3　いろいろな 食べ物が 海外から 来て、日本の スタイルに なりました。
Various other foods were brought from overseas and developed in the Japanese style.

1　12th to 13th Century　　2　Edo Period　　3　Meiji Period onward

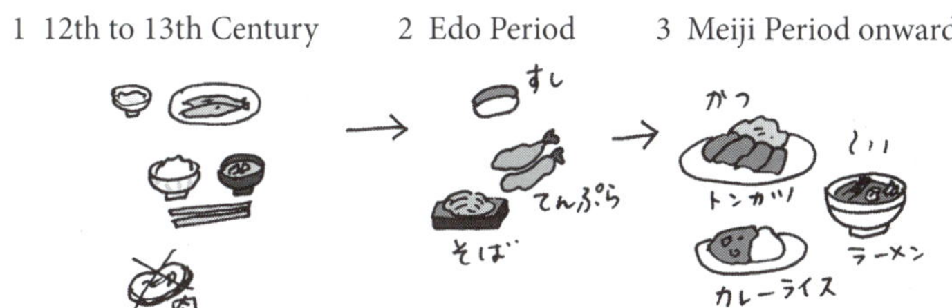

習慣　Customs

食べる前と 後は あいさつを します。宗教的な ことでは ありません。食べ物と 料理 を した 人への 感謝です。

Itadakimasu and *gochisousama deshita* are said before and after eating, respectively. These are not religious expressions, but instead show appreciation for the food and its preparation.

悪いマナー　Bad manners

さしばし	skewering food with chopsticks
よせばし	pulling dishes toward you with chopsticks
おそうしき	stabbing chopsticks in the rice (only used at funerals)
ふりまわす	gesturing with chopsticks

お箸が 苦手な 人は フォークやナイフ、スプーンを 使っても だいじょうぶです。
If you aren't good at using chopsticks, you can use a fork and knife or a spoon.

Meals at ryokan, hotels, and private lodging

日本の 旅館や 民宿では、伝統的な 日本 料 理が 出ます。たいてい 焼き魚と ごはんです。
朝、魚を 食べたくない 人は 喫茶店の モーニングサービスが おすすめです。

Ryokan (Japanese inns) and private lodging serve traditional foods, generally rice and grilled fish. If you don't want to eat fish in the morning, having breakfast at a café is recommended.

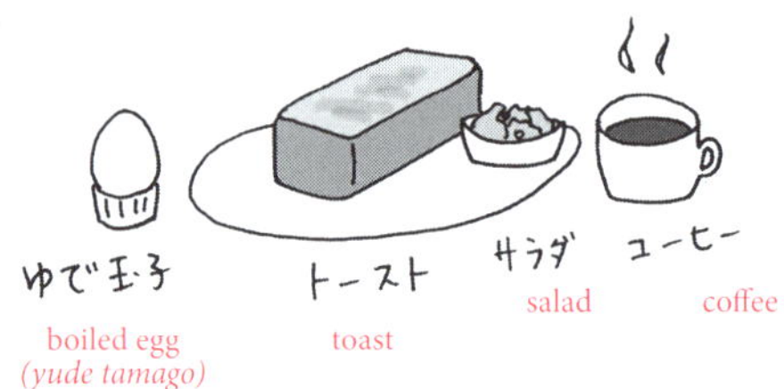

boiled egg
(*yude tamago*)   toast   salad   coffee

また、ホテルでは、Buffet-style の 朝ごはんも 人気です。「Buffet」は、フランス語の ように「ビュッフェ」と 発音します。

Buffet-style breakfasts are also popular in hotels. The word 'buffet' is pronounced *byuffe*, similar to how it is in French.

ビュッフェの食べ物の例 Typical foods at a buffet

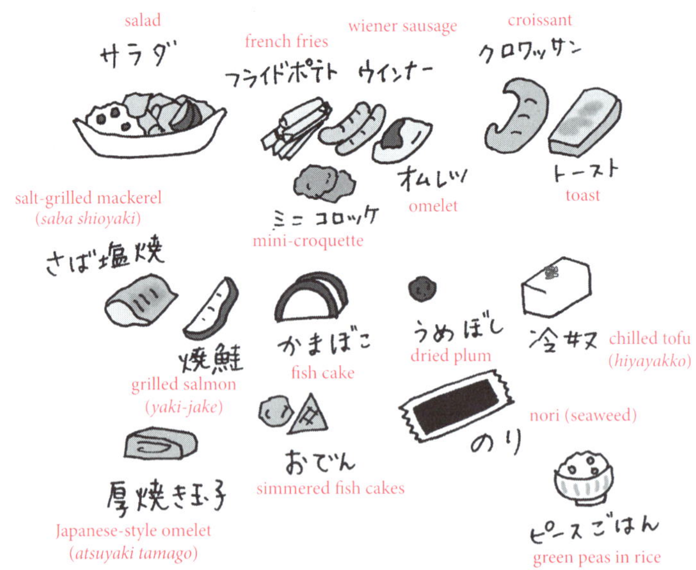

salad
french fries
wiener sausage
croissant
salt-grilled mackerel (*saba shioyaki*)
mini-croquette
omelet
toast
grilled salmon (*yaki-jake*)
fish cake
dried plum
chilled tofu (*hiyayakko*)
nori (seaweed)
Japanese-style omelet (*atsuyaki tamago*)
simmered fish cakes
green peas in rice

「ビュッフェ」を「バイキング」と 呼ぶことも よく あります。
北欧式ビュッフェ「スモーガスボード」を 日本で 始めたとき、「スモーガスボード」が 長くて 覚えにくかったので、映画「バイキング」から 名前を つけました。

Buffets are also referred to as *baikingu* ('Viking'). This is because a Japanese man created a Scandinavian-style buffet meal, but the word *smörgåsbord* was too hard to pronounce. So he named the meal after some Vikings he saw in a movie.

ビュッフェ／バイキングのマナー　Manners at a *baikingu*

食べ物は 残さないように します。料理を 少し 残したほうが マナーが いい という 人が いますが、それは 失礼です。

Eat all the food you take on your plate. Some say leaving a little food is polite, but this is not good etiquette.

注意！　Be careful!

日本料理は 魚の だしが 多いので、ベジタリアンと ヴィーガンの 人は 気をつけてください。店の人に 魚のだしを 使っているか どうか 聞いたほうが いいです（189〜191ページを 見てください）。

I'm vegetarian.

Most Japanese cuisine uses broth made from fish, so be careful if you are vegetarian or vegan. It's best to ask the staff if they use fish broth (see pages 189 through 191).

I wonder if miso soup is okay?

そばの食べ<ruby>食<rt>た</rt></ruby>べかた

How to eat soba

*https://matcha-jp.com/easy/9356

中国では、あまり 冷たい 麺を 食べません。林は、日本の 冷たい そばは お いしい と聞きました。

おそば屋さんに 行きましたが、食べかたが わかりません。どうしたら いい でしょうか。

In China, chilled noodles are not common. Rin heard that Japanese chilled noodles are good.
He's gone to a soba restaurant, but doesn't know the proper way to eat the noodles. What should he do?

"I wanna try some chilled soba."

"Here's your zaru soba!"   "Weird…"
"T-this…?"   "Oh! Sir!"

そばの<ruby>食<rt>た</rt></ruby>べかた
How to eat soba

1. Pour the soup.

2. Take some soba in your chopsticks.

3. Dip the noodles in the soup (dipping about one-third of the noodles is recommended).

めんつゆは「そばちょこ」という カップに 入れます。カップを 持ち上げて、少し とった そばを めんつゆに つけます。食べるときは、音を 立てて すすります。それは、しんせんな そばを 早く 食べている ことを 表すので、おいしそうに 食べて いる という 意味に なります。

Pour the soup (*mentsuyu*) into the cup (it's called a *sobachoko*). Hold it up then scoop some soba and dip. When you eat, slurp the noodles noisily! This shows the chef that you are eating the fresh noodles fast because they are delicious.

ねぎと わさびが、そばと いっしょに 来ます。つゆに 入れてもいいし、そばに のせても いいです。わさびは からいので、すこしずつ 入れたほうが いいですよ。

Soba is served with green onions and wasabi. You can put them in the soup or on the soba. Wasabi is very spicy, so don't overdo it!

和食の食べかた　How to eat Washoku

お寿司　Sushi

ほとんどの 人は 箸で 食べますが、実は 昔は 手で 食べました。今は、どちらでも だいじょうぶです。

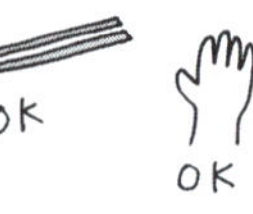

Most people eat sushi with chopsticks, but eating with one's hands was actually common in the past. Nowadays, either way is fine.

シャリ（酢の 味の ごはん）に しょうゆを つけません。
Don't put *shari* (vinegared rice) in soy sauce.

ネタ（魚）と シャリを 別々に しません。
Don't separate the *neta* (fish) and the *shari*.

ネタを 下に して、一口で 食べます。
Flip the sushi so the fish is on the bottom, then put the whole thing in your mouth.

ちらしずし（ネタを シャリに 散らした 寿司）は、ネタを しょうゆに つけて、また ごはんの 上に 戻して 食べます。

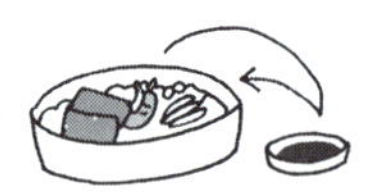

For *chirashizushi* ("scattered sushi"), take the neta and dip it in soy sauce, place it back on the rice, then eat it.

焼き魚　Grilled Fish

最初に 皮と 大きな 骨を とると 食べやすいです。よく 焼いた 皮は おいしいので 食べてみてください。頭が ついている 魚は、手で 頭を 軽く 押さえると 骨を とるのが 簡単です。

Getting rid of the skin and backbone makes the fish easier to eat. The crispy skin is delicious—you should try it! If the fish has a head, holding it with your other hand can help.

切り身　fillet　　丸ごと　whole

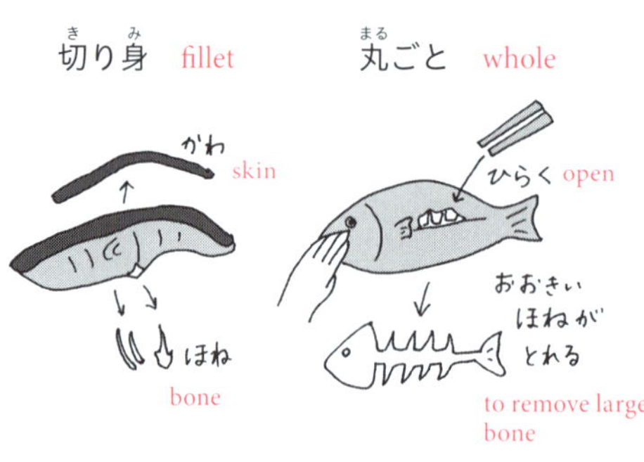

鍋 Hot pot

日本では、テーブルの 上に 鍋を 置いて、料理を しながら 食べるのが 人気です。鍋には いろいろな ものを 入れます。

In Japan, putting a *nabe* (pot) on the table and cooking while eating is popular. Many different ingredients can be placed in the pot.

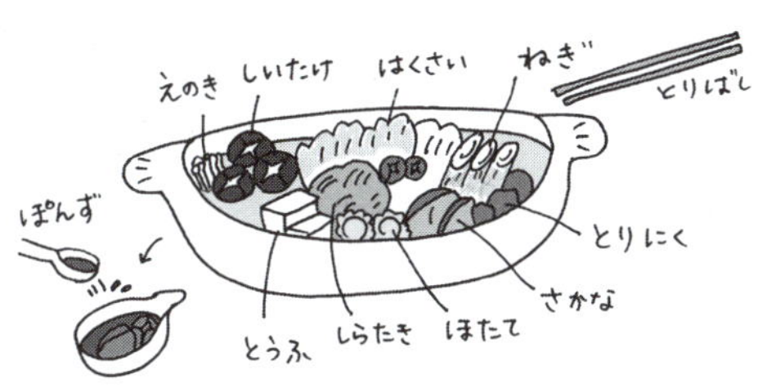

ponzu - a citrus-based sauce
enoki, shiitake - mushrooms
hakusai - napa cabbage
negi - green onions
toriniku - chicken
sakana - fish
hotate - scallops
shirataki - noodles
tofu - tofu

小さい ボウルに とって 食べます。家族や グループ みんなで 食べるときは、取り箸 と いう 長い箸を 使います。

Transfer the food into a small bowl to eat it. When dining with a group or family, use long chopsticks called *toribashi* to transfer the contents.

鍋の 中の スープだけでも おいしいですが、ポン酢 という すっぱい タレを つける 人も います。

The soup in the nabe is delicious on its own, but some people also add *ponzu*, a dipping sauce with a tart flavor.

しゃぶしゃぶ Shabu Shabu

お湯の 中に とても 薄い肉と 野菜を 入れます。そして、たれに つけて 食べます。ごまだれが 人気です。

Shabu shabu consists of thinly sliced meat and vegetables boiled in water then dipped in sauces and eaten. Sesame-seed sauce is popular with this dish.

すき焼き Sukiyaki

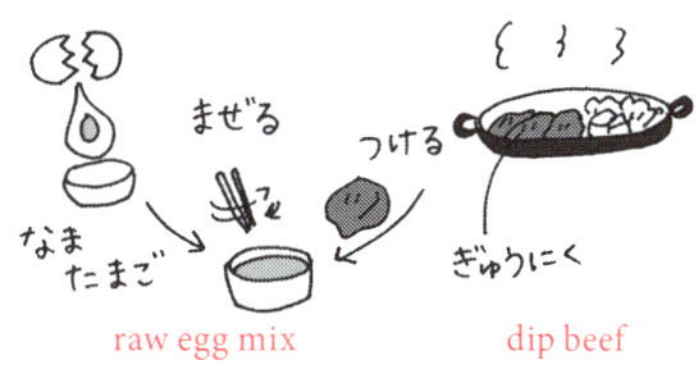

牛肉、野菜、豆腐、こんにゃくを しょうゆと 砂糖で 煮た 鍋です。よく 混ぜた 生卵に、牛肉や 野菜を つけて 食べます。

Sukiyaki is made by simmering beef, vegetables, tofu, and konnyaku in soy sauce and sugar. Most people dip the ingredients in a well-mixed raw egg before eating them.

鍋の 種類ですが、ほとんどの 材料は 魚の すり身で、しょう油と だしで 長い 時間 煮ます。コンビニにも あって、気軽に おやつとして 食べられます。

Oden is a type of nabe. Its primary ingredient is fish cakes, which are simmered for a long time in soy sauce and Japanese broth. Also sold at convenience stores, the dish can be eaten as a light snack.

他にも だいこんや こんぶ、ゆで卵などが あります。からしを つけて 食べると おいしいです。

Other ingredients include *daikon*, *konbu*, and boiled egg. *Karashi* (a spicy mustard with a horseradish taste) is good with it.

お好み焼き　Okonomiyaki

パンケーキみたい ですが、甘くない です。キャベツや 肉を 入れます。簡単な 料理なので、レストランでも、自分で 焼いて 楽しみます。

Okonomiyaki looks like a pancake, but it isn't sweet. It has cabbage and meat in it. Since the meal is simple to make, some restaurants even let you cook it yourself.

手巻き寿司　*Temakizushi*

家族や 友達と 家で お寿司を 作るときは、手巻き寿司 という かんたんな 寿司が 人気です。のりの 上に ごはんと 好きな 具を 入れて 巻きます。

Temakizushi is a simple and popular way of making sushi together with family and friends. Put rice and your favorite ingredients on top of a piece of *nori* (seaweed), then wrap it up.

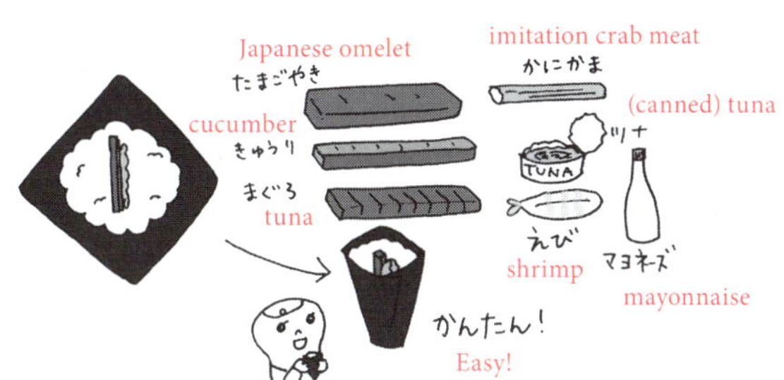

流しそうめん　*Nagashi sōmen*

そうめんは とても 細い 麺で、味は うどんと 同じです。流しそうめんは、長い 竹の 中に、そうめんを 冷たい 水で 流します。それを 取って 食べます。たいてい、夏に 山の 地方の レストランなどで 楽しみますが、家用の 機械も あります。

Sōmen are very thin noodles with a taste similar to udon. With *nagashi sōmen*, the noodles flow down a bamboo chute amidst ice-cold water. People then retrieve the noodles from the chute and eat them. *Nagashi sōmen* is generally enjoyed during the summer in restaurants in mountainous locales, but there are also devices that allow people to eat it at home.

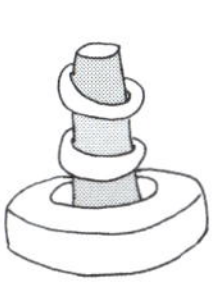

わんこそば　*Wanko soba*

店の人が 小さな お椀の 中に 少しだけ そばを 入れて、食べ終わると すぐ また そばを 入れます。店の人は「はい、じゃんじゃん」と 言いながら、お客さんが お椀の ふたを するまで 入れ続けます。岩手県の 名物です。

Wanko soba involves an attendant serving a small portion of soba noodles into your bowl; immediately after you eat them, she then serves you another portion. The attendant keeps serving while chanting phrases such as *Hai jan jan* as a way of encouraging you to eat more. The process continues until you put the lid on your bowl. Wanko soba is a specialty of Iwate Prefecture.

ごみの捨<ruby>す</ruby>てかた
Disposing of garbage

日本には、いろいろな 種類の ごみ箱が あります。ラジープが、会社の ごみ箱に 紙を 捨てているとき、先輩の 高橋さんが 来て、ラジープに ごみの 捨てかたを 教えました。

In Japan, there are various types of trash receptacles. Rajeep is throwing away some trash when his senior colleague Takahashi comes by and teaches him the proper way to dispose of trash.

[Rajeep throws some trash into the box that says "bin."]

"I know."
"That one is for *bin* (bottles)."

"Huh? You know?
  Then why (did you throw that in it)?"

"This goes in the bin."

「Bin」 と 「ビン」
English "bin" versus Japanese *bin*

日本語で「ビン」は、bottle の いみです。英語の Bin と ちがいます。ビンは、燃えないごみ（または 不燃ごみ）に 入れます。

紙などは、「燃えるごみ」または「可燃ごみ」と 言います。

In Japanese, *bin* means bottle, which is a lot different than the English word! Bottles go into the receptacles for unburnable trash.

Burnable trash such as paper is disposed of in receptacles marked *moeru gomi* or *kanen*.

日本語	英語
可燃 (燃えるごみ)	burnable
不燃 (燃えないごみ)	unburnable
ビン	bottles
カン	cans
ペットボトル	plastic bottles

"Burnable garbage is *kanen*.
Bottles are *bin*."

ごみについて　About garbage

それぞれの 市や 町には、ごみを 捨てる ための 袋が あります。袋には 町の 名前とごみ の 種類が 書いてあります。家の 外や マンションの 地下には ごみの 袋を 置く 場所が あ ります。

Every city or town has designated bags for disposing of garbage. These bags are labeled with both the name of the town or city and the type of garbage. Collection areas for the bags can be found near the street in residential areas or in the subfloors of apartment buildings.

可燃（燃えるごみ）
burnable garbage

不燃（燃えないごみ）
unburnable garbage

リサイクルごみ **Recyclables**

リサイクルの ための 袋に 入れるか、町の リサイクルセンターに 持って行きます。市に よって、リサイクルできるものは 違います。

Use a special recycling bag or bring your recyclables to a recycle center in your town. Each city has different rules for what items can be recycled.

また、ほとんどのスーパーにはリ サイクルのための箱があります。

Most supermarkets also have receptacles for recycling.

大きな ごみは お金を はらわなければいけません。たいてい、市役所に 電話を して、チケットを 買います。そして、その チケットを ごみに 貼って、指定された 場所に おきます。

To dispose of oversized garbage items, you'll have to pay a fee by calling the city office and buying a ticket. Attach the ticket to the item then place it in the designated location.

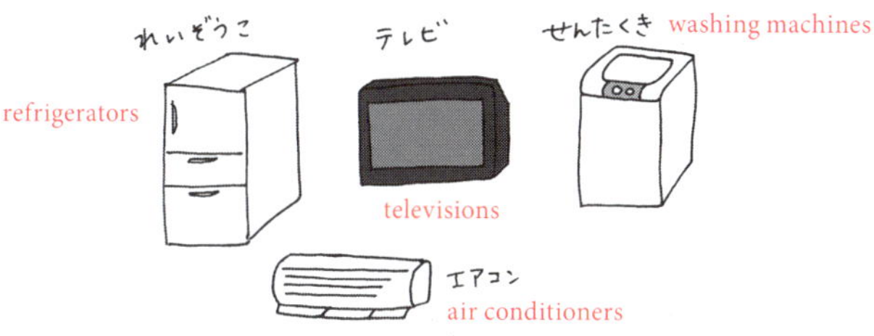

＊町によって 方法が 違います。かならず 確認してください。

Every town has different rules, so be sure to check with your local officials first.

旅行中のごみ Disposing of trash when traveling

日本には、外に ごみ箱が ありません。ごみ箱に 危ないものを 入れないように する ためです。お店で 食べ物を 買った後、ごみを 捨てたい 場合は、店に もどって「捨ててくれますか？」と 聞いてみてください。

In Japan, there are no trash cans outside. This is to prevent dangerous items from being left in them. If you need to dispose of some trash after eating food from a shop, return to the shop and ask them if you can throw it away (*sutete kuremasu ka*?).

店で 捨てることが できない場合は、ホテルや 旅館で 捨ててください。

If you can't dispose of the trash at the shop, bring it to your hotel or inn.

＊https://matcha-jp.com/en/10149

無料のWi-Fi スポット　Free Wi-Fi spots

日本には、無料のWi-Fi スポット が たくさん あります。さらに 充電 も できる ところも いくつか あります。

Japan has a lot of free Wi-Fi spots. Many of them also have places where you can charge your phone.

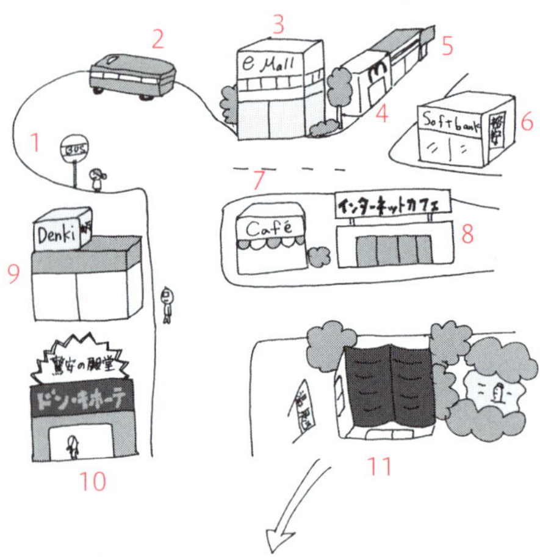

1. バス停 Bus stops
2. バス Buses
3. ショッピングモール Shopping malls
4. ファーストフード Fast-food restaurants
5. コンビニ Convenience stores
6. スマホの店 Smartphone shops
7. 喫茶店 Coffee shops
8. ネットカフェ、マンガ喫茶 Internet cafés and manga cafés
9. 大型家電店 Electronics retailers
10. ドン・キホーテ Don Quijote (discount chain store)
11. 温泉 Hot-spring spas

日本でのマナー　Good manners in Japan

温泉　Onsen

着替える 場所で 大きい 声で 笑ったり 話したり しないでください。

Don't talk or laugh loudly in dressing rooms.

髪が 長い 人は 髪を ゴムなどで まとめてください。

If you have long hair, keep it tied up.

お風呂に 入る 前は 体を 洗ってください。

Wash your body before getting in a public bath.

お風呂に タオルを 入れないでください。
たいてい 女の人は タオルを お風呂の 端に 置きます。

Don't put your towel in the bath. Most women place their towel on the edge.

男 の人は 頭の 上に 置きます。メガネを かけたまま お風呂に 入って
も だいじょうぶです。

Men place their towels on their heads.
You can wear your glasses in the bath.

お風呂の 中で 泳がないでください。

Don't swim in the bath.

トイレ　Restrooms

日本には、2種類の トイレが あります。洋式と 和
式です。右の 絵のように 座って 使ってください。

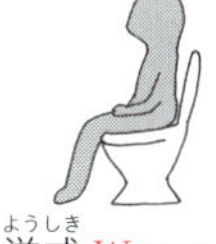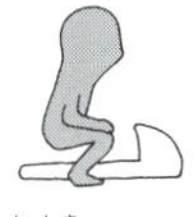

洋式 Western　　和式 Japanese

In Japan, there are two types of toilets: Western style
and Japanese style. Sit on them as depicted in the drawing on the right.

伝統的な場所　Traditional places

京都では 舞妓さんが 仕事に 行く ために
歩いています。舞妓さんに 触ったり、写
真を とったり しないでください。舞妓さ
んが 困ってしまいます。

In Kyoto, you can see *maiko* (apprentice geisha) walking to work. Please don't
touch them or take pictures. That is very troublesome for them.

人が 多い ところでは 食べながら 歩かないで
ください。

Don't eat while walking around crowded places.

防災

ぼうさい

Disaster prevention

クリスティーヌは 町の コミュニティーセンターの 前を 通ったとき、男の人に 水と お菓子を もらいました。缶には「防災」と 書いてあります。クリスティーヌは、「防災」の いみが よく わかりません。

When Christine passed by her town's community center, a man gave her a bottle of water and a canned snack. The word 防災 (*bōsai*) was written on the can, but she doesn't know what it means.

"I got Bōsai snacks and a bottle of water."
"Me too."

"These are hard, but tasty!" <crunch crunch>
"Don't eat them now!"

災害からの被害を防ぐために
Preventing damage during a disaster

日本には、災害（地震、津波、台風など）が たくさん あります。防災とは、「災害の 被害を防ぐ」という意味です。

Japan has a lot of disasters such as earthquakes, tsunamis, and typhoons. These are known as *saigai*. *Bōsai* means to prevent damage during a disaster (*bō* means "prevent" in Japanese).

日本の 政府は、9月1日を「防災の日」と 決めました。その日は、避難訓練（逃げる ための 練習）を したり、食べ物や 水を 準備したり します。

The Japanese government has designated September 1st as "Disaster Prevention Day." On this day, evacuation drills are conducted and emergency food and water is distributed.

いくつかの 市や 町では、無料で 食べ物や 水を みんなに あげます。おいしそうですが、食べないで とっておいてください。

In some cities and towns, residents are given emergency food and water free of charge. Although these items might look tasty, please save them for emergency situations.

"Save them for an emergency!"

その他の防災グッズ　Other emergency goods

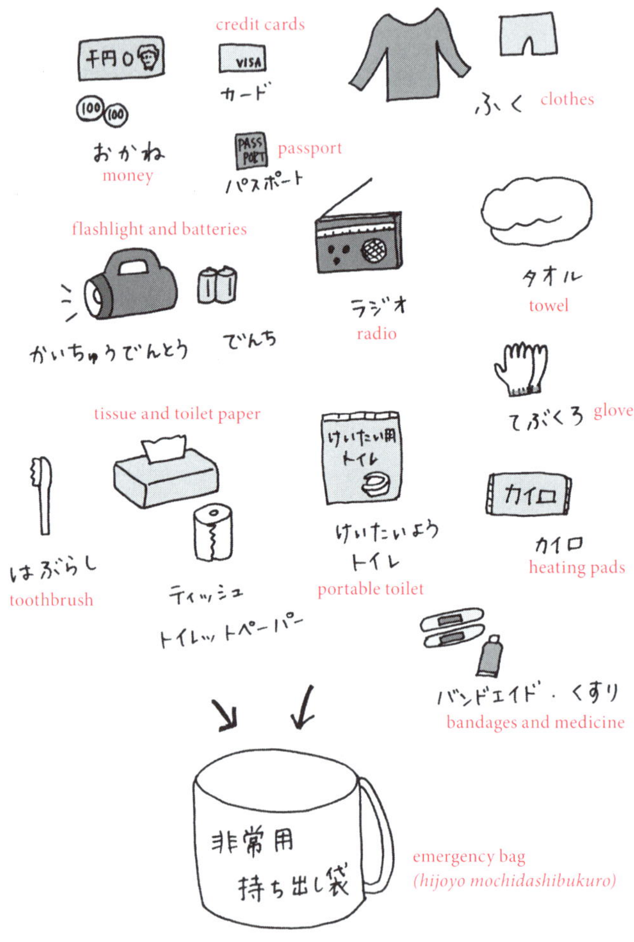

これらの ものを 袋に 入れて、安全な 場所に おいておけば、災害が 起きたときに すぐに 使うことが できます。

Place these items in a bag and store them in a safe place so that they are available if a disaster strikes.

避難所　Evacuation shelters

近くの コミュニティーセンターや 学校が 避難所に なります。

A community center or school nearby will be set up as an evacuation shelter.

避難所では、市や 町の 人が 外国人を 助けてくれるので、心配しないでください。

City officials will provide assistance to foreigners at evacuation shelters, so don't worry.

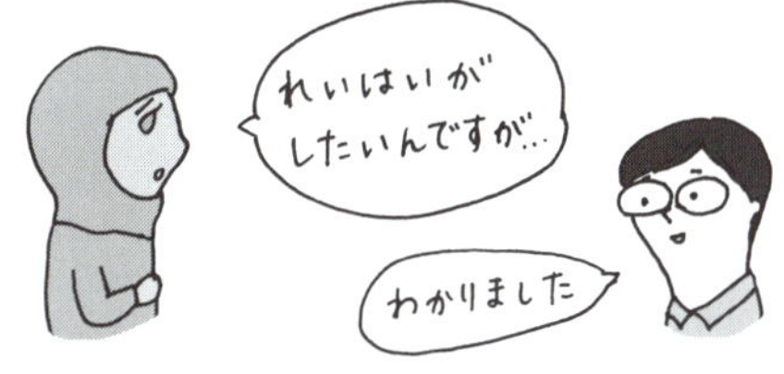

"I'd like to pray…"

"Alright."

災害用伝言板171　Disaster emergency board (web171)

災害の ときは、たくさんの 人が 心配して 電話と インターネットを使うので、つながりにくく なります。171は、あなたが 音声 または テキストで メッセージを 送って、家族や ともだちが その メッセージを 聞いたり 見たり することが できる サービスです。無料 で使えます。

When a disaster strikes, many people will be worriedly using the telephone and Internet, making it difficult to connect. Web171 is a service that allows people to record audio or text messages so that their loved ones can verify their safety during a disaster. It is free to use.

*https://www.ntt-west.co.jp/dengon/web171/english/

"I'm okay!"

地震
Earthquakes

日本（に ほん）は 地震（じ しん）が たくさん あります。そして、地震（じ しん）は いつ 起（お）きるか わかりません。林（りん）が 料理（りょうり）を しているとき、急（きゅう）に 地震（じ しん）が 起（お）きました。林（りん）は、びっくりして、火（ひ）を 消（け）さないで、外（そと）に 出（で）てしまいました。

Japan has many earthquakes, and there is no way to know when one might occur. Rin was cooking a meal when an earthquake struck suddenly. Startled, Rin runs out of his apartment without turning off the stove.

<rattling and shaking>

<panicking>

"Help!"

地震が起きたとき
When an earthquake occurs

地震が 起きたときは、外に でないで、テーブルの 下など、体が 守れる ところに 行ってください。

If you sense an earthquake, don't rush outside. Get under something that can protect your body, such as a table.

まんがでは、ガスコンロの 火で、火事に なって しまいましたが、最近の ガスコンロは、揺れ始めたら 止まるように なっていますから、だいじょうぶです。

In the manga, the flame from the gas burner started a fire. However, newer gas stoves are equipped with sensors that turn them off when vibration is detected.

もし 火が ついたときは、まず、「かじです！」と 大きな 声で 近くの 人に 言って ください。そして、できれば 消火器や 水で 火を 消してください。できなかった ら、避難してください。

If a fire breaks out, yell *Kaji desu!* ("There's a fire!") to notify the neighbors. If possible, extinguish the fire with water or a fire extinguisher; otherwise, evacuate the area.

"The flame went out!"

Stop!

"It's OK now!"

地震のとき、もし○○にいたら…？
Reacting to earthquakes when you are...

屋外 Outside

外は いろいろな 物が 落ちてきて 危ないです。道の 真ん中に
行ってください。そして、頭を なにかで守ってください。

Being outside during an earthquake is dangerous because objects can fall on you. If you must go out, walk in the center of the street and cover your head with something to protect it.

エレベーターの中 In an elevator

地震が 起きたら、すぐに 全部の 階の ボタンを 押して、最初に ドアが
開いた 階で 降りてください。エレベーターは 地震が あると 止まるので、
エレベーターの 外に 出られなくなります。もし 外に 出られない場合は、
非常ボタンを 押して、助けを 待ってください。

If an earthquake occurs while you are riding in an elevator, immediately press the buttons for all floors then exit the elevator as soon as the door opens. Elevators are designed to stop operating during earthquakes, so you might get stuck inside it. If you are trapped in an elevator, press the emergency button and wait for help.

電車の中 In a train

駅員さんが 安全な ところに 案内しますから、あわてないで 待ってください。

Don't panic! Wait until a train worker directs passengers to a safe location.

山の近く Near a mountain

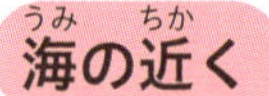

大きな 石が 落ちるかもしれません。「落石 注意」の 標識を よく 見てください。

Beware of large stones falling. Pay close attention to signs that indicate such danger.

海の近く Near the ocean

大きな 地震の 後には 津波が 来ることが あります。高い ところに 逃げてください。

Large earthquakes can create tsunamis. Evacuate to a higher elevation.

震度とマグニチュード　Shindo (seismic intensity) and magnitude

マグニチュードは 地震の 大きさです。震度は あなたの いる 場所の 揺れの 大きさです。

Magnitude refers to the power of the earthquake itself, whereas *shindo* indicates the vibration at your location.

マグニチュードが 大きいけど 遠い

Large magnitude but far away, so the *shindo* is low.

マグニチュードが 小さいけど 近い

Small magnitude but nearby, so the *shindo* is high.

震度の大きさ　The shindo scale

震度は 7まで 大きさが あります。　The shindo scale has seven levels.

津波
Tsunami

ラジープが 会社の 事務所で 仕事を しているとき、大きな 地震が ありました。そして 地震が 終わった後、ニュースで 津波が 来ることを 知りました。ラジープは 車で 高いところに 行こう と 思いましたが……。

When Rajeep was working at the company's office, a powerful earthquake struck. After it stopped, he learned from the news that a tsunami was coming. Rajeep decides to drive to higher ground.

<after an earthquake> tsunami warning
"Tsunami?!"

"This...and this...
(Should be OK since I'm driving.)"

"This is slow!"

"Hurry!!"

津波が近づいているとき
When a tsunami is coming

津波は とても 速いです。海の 深い ところから、飛行機の ような 速さで やってきます。いろいろな ものを 持って行きたい と思っても、大切な もの（ID、携帯電話など）だけを 持って、逃げてください。

Tsunami move very quickly. They travel from the open ocean with the speed of an airplane. Although you might want to take many things with you, just grab the most important items (your ID, mobile phone, etc.) and evacuate immediately.

車を 運転するよりも、走ったほうが いいです。2011年の 大きな 津波では、車が道に たくさん 止まって、大勢の 人が 死んでしまいました。

Running is better than driving a vehicle. During the major tsunami in 2011, many people died because they got stuck in heavy traffic on the roadways.

そして、遠い ところ よりも、高い ところのほうが いいです。できるだけ、山の上や 津波タワーに 行ってください。

Also, getting to higher elevation is better than getting far away. Climb to the top of a mountain or tsunami tower if possible.

津波について　About tsunami

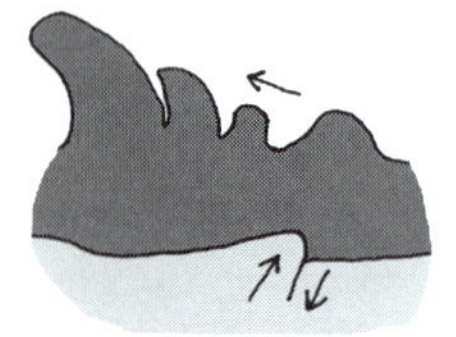

津波は、海の 底が 動いて 起こります。

Tsunami are generated when the seafloor moves.

津波が１mから３mの場合は、とても 危ないので、「津波警報」が でます。

Tsunami that are 1 to 3 meters high are extremely dangerous, so a tsunami warning is issued when they are detected.

10mより 大きい 津波は「大津波警報」です。家も 人も 流されてしまいます。2011年の 大きな 地震のとき、一番 大きい 津波は40mでした。

For tsunami higher than 10 meters, a major tsunami warning (the most severe) is issued. These powerful waves can wash away both houses and people. After the massive earthquake in 2011, the tallest tsunami measured 40 meters.

海に いるときに 津波が 起きたときは、赤と 白の 大きな 旗が でます。もし、その 旗を 見たら、すぐに 浜に もどって、高い ところに 逃げてください。

If a tsunami occurs while you are in the water, a large red and white flag will be displayed. When you see this flag, return to the beach immediately and evacuate to a higher elevation.

津波は1回では ありません。だいじょうぶだ と思って、海に 戻るのは、とても 危険です。

Tsunami are not always a single event; the same earthquake can produce multiple waves. Returning to the ocean because you think it is safe is very dangerous.

川や 海に 行ったときは、津波 注意の 標識が あるか どうか、よく 見てください。

If you go to a river or beach, pay attention to whether there is a tsunami warning sign.

↑ 津波が 来たときに 逃げる ための 建物には、マークが あります。

Buildings that are designated as tsunami evacuation sites display signs denoting their status.

<ruby>朝<rt>あさ</rt></ruby> スリが <ruby>窓<rt>まど</rt></ruby>を <ruby>開<rt>あ</rt></ruby>けると、<ruby>外<rt>そと</rt></ruby>は とても いい <ruby>天気<rt>てんき</rt></ruby>だったので、<ruby>電車<rt>でんしゃ</rt></ruby>に <ruby>乗<rt>の</rt></ruby>って <ruby>買<rt>か</rt></ruby>い<ruby>物<rt>もの</rt></ruby>に <ruby>行<rt>い</rt></ruby>きました。でも、<ruby>帰<rt>かえ</rt></ruby>ろうと したとき、<ruby>強<rt>つよ</rt></ruby>い <ruby>風<rt>かぜ</rt></ruby>と <ruby>雨<rt>あめ</rt></ruby>で <ruby>電車<rt>でんしゃ</rt></ruby>が <ruby>止<rt>と</rt></ruby>まってしまいました。

When Suri opened the window in the morning, she saw the beautiful weather and decided to take the train to go shopping. On her way home, however, the train was out of service due to strong winds and rain.

"Beautiful weather! I'll go shopping in Shibuya."

"There are only a few people today? Hmm?"

two hours later <wind blowing furiously>
"Oh my! But it was such nice weather."

"What should I do...? I can't get home..."

台風が近づいているとき
When a typhoon is coming

日本では、毎年9月から10月は台風がたくさん来ます。台風のときは、朝、天気が良くても、急に悪くなります。天気予報とニュースを見て、台風が来そうなときは出かけないようにしてください。

Every September and October, Japan experiences a lot of typhoons. This can make the weather quickly change for the worse, even if it was nice in the morning. Be sure to check the weather forecast and news before heading out; if a typhoon is likely to come, stay at home.

台風の目にいるときは晴れています。でもその後にまた強い風と雨があります。台風が来ると電車やバスが止まってしまうことがあります。

The weather is clear in the eye or center of a typhoon, but once it passes, strong winds and heavy rain will appear again. Bus and train services are sometimes suspended when a typhoon is coming.

この場合、24時間あいている店を探したほうがいいです。そこで台風がおわるまで待つことができます。インターネットカフェ、ファミリーレストラン、サウナなどは、24時間あいていることが多いです。

In such cases, try to find a store that is open 24 hours a day where you can wait out the storm. This includes most Internet cafés, family restaurants, and saunas.

Open 24 hours

台風が来る前に　Before a typhoon comes

ベランダや 庭の 高い ところに あるものは、下に おいてください。
Lower any items that are placed in high locations on your veranda or in your yard.

←洗濯ものの ための 長い 棒　long bar for hanging laundry

←鉢植え　flower pots

窓から 雨が 入ったり、強い 風で 窓が 割れるかもしれません。テープを 貼るといいです。

There is a possibility that rain will seep through the window or strong wind will break it. To prevent this, attach tape to the edges and center to strengthen the window.

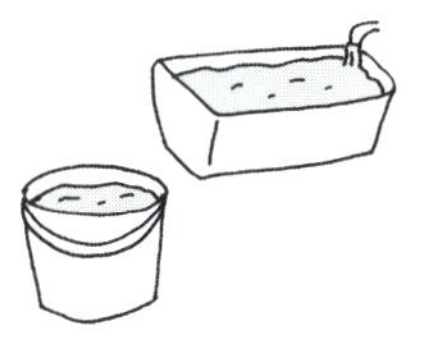

水が 止まるかもしれません。水を ためておいてください。

Also, your water service might be suspended. Fill a bathtub or bucket with water just in case.

電気が 止まるかもしれません。懐中電灯と 電池を 用意して、スマートフォンは 充電しておいてください。

You might not have power, either, so prepare a flashlight with batteries and charge your smartphone.

台風は 暑い 季節に 来ます。クーラーボックスに 保冷剤、氷が あると、もっと いいです。
Typhoon season is a hot time of year, so it's best to put some ice or ice packs in a chest cooler.

台風が来たときは　When a typhoon hits

家に いるときに 台風が 来たら、外に 出ないように し
てください。外の 物が 倒れたり、飛んできたりします。
大雨に なるときも あります。できるだけ、家の中の 高
いところに 行ってください。

If a typhoon arrives when you are at home, don't go
outside. Things could break and fall, and objects may be
flying around. Heavy rains can also occur. If possible,
head to a higher location in your house.

⇒旅行のときは どうする？　What if you are on vacation?

台風のとき、電車、飛行機、バスなどの 公共 交通機関が 止まってしまいます。ま
た、ツアーなども キャンセルに なるでしょう。電話や インターネットで 確認し
てください。

When a typhoon hits, transportation such as trains, flights, and buses will be
suspended. Tours will also be canceled. Use your phone or the Internet to obtain
information about these services.

「○○は キャンセルですか？
お金は かえしてもらえますか？」
と 聞いてください。

You can ask:

○○ *wa kyanseru desu ka? Okane wa
kaeshite moraemasu ka?*

("Has ○○ been canceled? Can I get a
refund?")

熱中症
ねっちゅうしょう

Heatstroke

日本の 夏は とても 暑いです。ラジープが 仕事のために 外に 行こうとしたので、同僚が 心配しました。でも、ラジープは インドから 来たので、暑さは だいじょうぶだ と思っています。

Japanese summers can be very hot. Rajeep is about to go outside for work, so his coworker is worried about him. But because he is from India, Rajeep thinks heat is not a problem for him.

"I'm going to Company B's office in Shinjuku."
"It's very hot, be careful (stay cool)."
"Haha. India is hot, too." "It's hot!"

"So thirsty... but I'm almost there..."

"He...llo..." <dizzy> <falls to the ground heavily>
"Oh no!"

熱中症にならないために
Preventing heatstroke

日本の 夏は とても 蒸し暑いです。気温は たいてい 30℃くらいですが、特に 東京は 人が 多いので 天気予報の 気温よりも 暑く 感じます。

Summer in Japan is very hot and humid. The air temperature is usually around 30 °C, but it can feel hotter—especially in Tokyo due to its enormous population.

だいじょうぶだ と思っても、たくさん 水を 飲んでください。水筒や ペットボトルに 水を 入れて、いつも 持っていったほうが いいです。汗が たくさん でたときは、塩分も 必要ですから、塩飴が おすすめです。

Drink plenty of water even if you think you're fine. It's best to put some water in a thermos or plastic bottle and always carry it with you. If you sweat a lot, you'll need to intake some salt as well, so some salty candy is recommended.

*https://matcha-jp.com/en/2772

熱中症とは　Signs of heatstroke

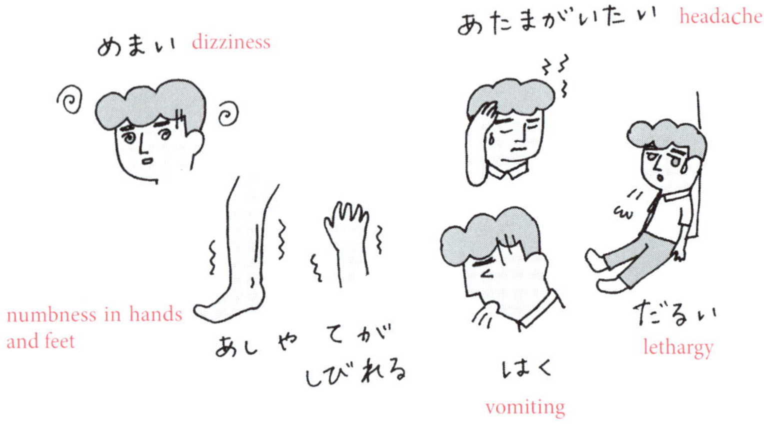

熱中症だ と感じたら、涼しい ところに 行って、体を 冷やしてください。

If you think you are experiencing heatstroke, head to a cooler location and cool down your body.

冷やしたほうがいいところ　Best areas to cool

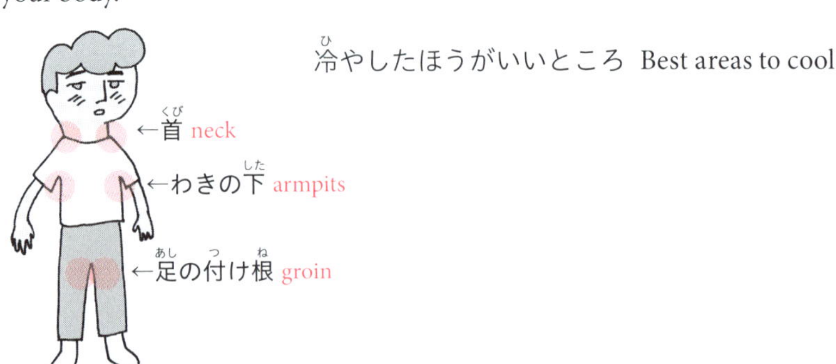

熱中症予防に便利なもの
Useful items for preventing heatstroke

経口補水液 という 飲み物が おすすめです。長い 時間 出かけるときは、ゼリータイプを 凍らせると いいです。

A drink known as oral rehydration solution is recommended. There is a frozen gel type if you will be outside for a long period of time.

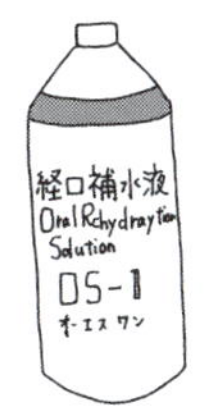

UV99％カットの 日傘
umbrella that blocks 99% UV

冷却スプレー
ice spray

冷却剤
ice pack

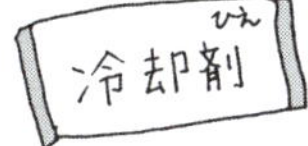

工事や 工場で 働く 人のために、ヘルメットの 中に 入れる 冷却剤が あります。冷却剤や 小さい 扇風機を 作業着の 中に 入れることも あります。

For construction and factory workers, there are ice packs made to fit inside safety helmets. There are even coolant packs and tiny fans that attach to work clothes.

部屋の 中に いても 熱中症に なることが あります。エアコンだけではなく、扇風機も 使うと いいです。

Even indoors, you are still at risk for heatstroke. Using an electric fan in addition to the AC is a good idea.

夏用の特別な UVカーテンと シーツも あります。

There are also special curtains and bedsheets for use in the summer.

大雪
Heavy snow

雪が たくさん 降りました。林が 外に 出たとき、ヒールの 高い ブーツを はいた 女の人が、道で 転びました。林は それを 見て 笑っていましたが……。

A lot of snow fell. When Rin went outside, a woman wearing high-heeled boots had slipped on the road. Rin is amused by her situation, but…

"Wearing boots like that is dangerous!"
<laughs>

"When it's snowing, rubber boots are the best!"

"Oh!"

"You have to watch what's above you, too…"
<giggles>

雪の上を歩くときは
When walking on snow

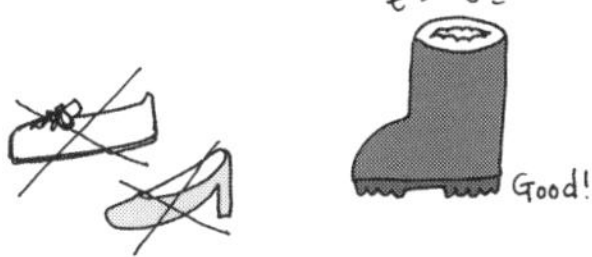

滑りにくい 靴を はいてください！

Don't wear slippery shoes!

高い ヒールの 靴や、裏が 平らな 靴は、滑りやすいので 危ないです。雪や 氷の 上を 歩くときは、裏が 凸凹している 靴を はいてください。特に、中が もこもこの 物は あたたかくて いいです。

High-heels and shoes with flat soles are slippery and dangerous. When walking on snow or ice, be sure to wear shoes that have rugged soles. Boots that are fluffy and warm inside are especially useful.

雪の ための 靴が ない 人や、買いたくない 人には、「スノースパイク」という バンドが おすすめです。かんたんに 靴に つけることが できます。急に 雪が 降って 買うことが できない場合は、輪ゴムを つけてください。

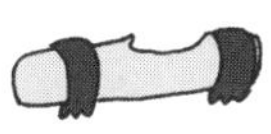

If you don't have shoes for snow and don't want to buy any, try the "snow spike" bands. They can be attached to your shoes easily. If snow falls unexpectedly and you are in a pinch, you can also wrap wide rubber bands around your shoes for some grip.

スノースパイクは アウトドアの 店や オンラインショップで 買うことができます。

Snow spikes can be purchased from outdoor retailers or online shops.

雪や 氷の 上は、ゆっくり、ペンギンのように、足の裏を 全部つけて、すこしずつ 歩いてください。

Walk slowly on snow or ice, like a penguin: take short, waddling steps rather than long strides, and place the soles of your feet evenly on the ground.

転んだときに、けがを しないように、手袋、帽子、厚いコートなどが おすすめです。

Wear gloves, a hat, and a thick coat to prevent serious injuries if you slip and fall.

雪がたくさん降るところ　The snowiest places in Japan

日本海（日本の西の海）の 地方と 北海道は ロシアから 冷たい 風が 来ます。とても 強くて寒いので、天気予報では「冬 将軍が 来る」と 言います。その 地方は、よく 大雪になります。

Areas bordering the Sea of Japan (to the country's west) as well as Hokkaido receive cold winds from Russia. This makes them extremely cold, so the weather forecast refers to their winters by saying that "General Winter is coming." These regions often experience heavy snowfall.

日本には、世界で 一番 雪が たくさん 降る 場所が いくつか あります。

Japan has some of the snowiest places on Earth.

←太平洋（日本の東の海）の 地方は あまり 雪が 降りません。1年に1、2回です。

Snow doesn't fall often on Japan's Pacific Coast (to the country's east). These regions see snow only one or two times a year.

長野 という 地域は 高い 山が たくさん あるので、雪が 多いです。

The region known as Nagano has many tall mountains which experience heavy snow.

雪の多いところに車で行くとき　Driving in heavy snow

雪用の タイヤを つけてください。雪用タイヤが ないときは、タイヤに チェーンを つけたほうが いいです。

Use snow tires when driving on snow. If you don't have snow tires, you should attach chains to your tires.

短い 時間や 緊急のときは、滑りにくくする スプレーが 便利です。

For very short periods or in an emergency, the liquid spray that helps your tires grip the road is convenient.

大雪で 車が 動かないとき、マフラーの 周りの 雪を とってください。車のガスが 中に 入って 危ないです。

If your car is stuck in deep snow, remove the snow from around the muffler. If you don't, the car's dangerous exhaust fumes could enter the car.

雪山に出かけたら　If on a snowy mountain

スキーや スノーボードに 行ったときは、危ないところには 行かないでください。

If you go skiing or snowboarding, avoid dangerous areas.

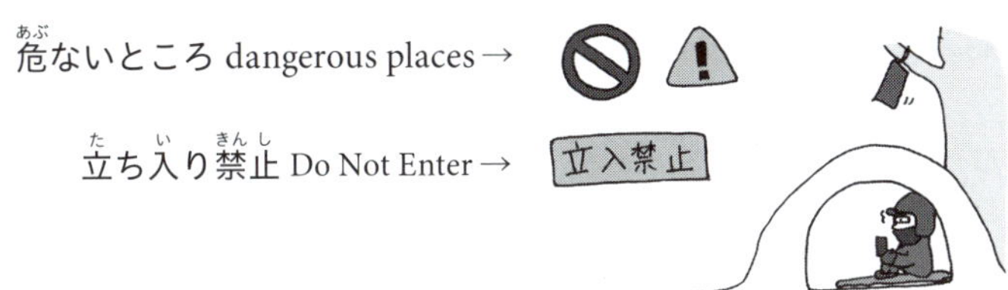

もし 雪山で 迷って、帰ることが できない場合は、雪を 掘って 穴を 作ってください。たくさん 歩くと 体力が なくなってしまいます。助けが 来るように 目立つ 色の 物（明るい色の タオルや 服）を 見えるところに つけてください。

If you get lost and stranded on a snowy mountain, dig a large hole in the snow. If you walk a lot trying to find your way out, you will run out of energy. Tie a conspicuous object (a brightly colored towel, article of clothing, etc.) somewhere it will be noticed.

*https://weathernews.jp/s/topics/201902/040205/

雪のときに便利な物　Useful items for snow

カイロ heat pad
靴の中用カイロ heat pad for shoes
耳当て earmuffs
耳当て付きの 帽子 hat with ear flaps
雪用の 手袋、靴とくつ下
snow gloves, shoes, and socks

雪で いろいろな ものが 凍ったときは、解氷スプレーが 便利です。
De-icer spray is handy when various objects have been frozen by the snow.

大雪で 電気が 止まってしまったときは、カセットコンロが とても 役に立ちます。

When heavy snow causes an electric outage, a portable stove can be a lifesaver.

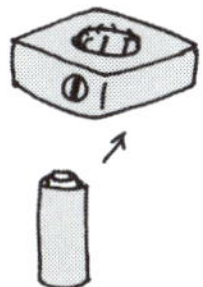

火山
Volcanoes

クリスティーヌは 山を 登っているとき、卵の くさったような、変な におい に 気がつきました。その後、空が 黒くなって、たくさんの 煙が 来ました。火山が 噴火しそうです。

Christine was climbing a mountain when she noticed a strange smell like rotten eggs. Soon after, the sky turned black and hazy. It seems that the volcano is erupting.

"Nice view!"

"Strange smell..."

"Oh! My eyes!"

"I can't see!"
<coughing>

山が噴火しそうなときは

When a volcano is about to erupt

変な においは、火山が 噴火（マグマが 山から出ること）するときの においです。たくさんの 灰も でます。火山灰と 言います。火山灰は 体に とても 悪いです。

A strange smell occurs when a volcano erupts (magma is ejected from it). A large amount of ash (*kazanbai*) is also released. Volcanic ash is very bad for your health.

目を 守るために、眼鏡や ゴーグルを 使ってください。コンタクトレンズを している場合は、とって ください。

Use glasses or goggles to protect your eyes. If you are wearing contact lenses, remove them.

喉が 痛くなったり、咳が 出たりします。ハンカチや タオルで 火山灰が 口と 鼻に 入らないように してください。

You might get a sore throat or start coughing. Cover your mouth and nose with a handkerchief or towel to prevent the ash from being inhaled.

ヘルメットを したほうが いいですが、ない場合は、バックパックで 頭を まもってください。そして、山小屋の 中に 入ってください。山小屋が ないときには、大きな 岩の 後ろなどに 行ってください。

It's best to wear a helmet; but if you don't have one, protect your head with your backpack. Also, try to make your way to a hut on the mountain for refuge. If there isn't one nearby, take cover behind a large rock.

登山のときの準備　Mountaineering preparation

日本には111の 火山が あります。火山は、いつ 噴火するか、わかりません。登りに 行くときには、火山警報を チェックしてください。

Japan has 111 volcanoes which could erupt at any time. Check for volcano warnings before going climbing on one of them.

＊https://www.jma.go.jp/bosai/map.html#5/34.5/137/&contents=volcano&lang=en

登山の 前に 計画書を 書いてください。英語でも だいじょうぶです。山の あるところの 警察署に 持って 行きますが、Email でも だいじょうぶです。

Before heading off to the mountain, make a climbing plan. Writing it in English is fine. You can then either bring or email it to a police station near the mountain.

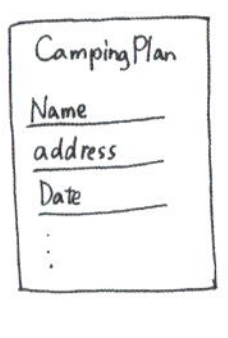

スマホの アプリで 計画書を ともだちと シェアしたり、山の 地図や 天気を 見ることも できます。

There is also a smartphone app that allows you to do things like share your climbing plan with friends and check the weather on the mountain.

＊https://www.mt-compass.com

登山の服と持ち物　What to wear and bring when mountaineering

サングラス sunglasses
日焼け止め sunscreen
軍手 work gloves
レインコート raincoat
つえ cane
とざんぐつ climbing boots
スマートフォン smartphone
おかし sweets, snacks
くすり medicine
ヘッドライト headlamp
みず water
タオル towel
ちず map

<ruby>登山<rt>とざん</rt></ruby>のときのマナー　Mountaineering manners

テントを <ruby>立<rt>た</rt></ruby>てたり、キャンプファイヤーを してはいけない <ruby>山<rt>やま</rt></ruby>が おおいです。しても いいか どうか、しらべて ください。

Things like pitching a tent and building a campfire are prohibited on many mountains. Be sure to research what is permitted before heading out.

<ruby>富士山<rt>ふじさん</rt></ruby>の ルールと マナーは こちらの リンクを <ruby>見<rt>み</rt></ruby>て ください。

The following link lists some rules and manners for Mount Fuji.

＊http://www.fujisan-climb.jp/en/todays/index.html

<ruby>登<rt>のぼ</rt></ruby>る <ruby>人<rt>ひと</rt></ruby>が <ruby>来<rt>き</rt></ruby>たら、<ruby>降<rt>お</rt></ruby>りる <ruby>人<rt>ひと</rt></ruby>は <ruby>道<rt>みち</rt></ruby>の <ruby>端<rt>はじ</rt></ruby>で <ruby>待<rt>ま</rt></ruby>って ください。

If you are descending the mountain and encounter someone who is on their way up, move to the edge of the road and let them pass before continuing.

ゴミを <ruby>捨<rt>す</rt></ruby>てないで ください。うちに <ruby>持<rt>も</rt></ruby>って <ruby>帰<rt>かえ</rt></ruby>って ください。また、<ruby>山<rt>やま</rt></ruby>の<ruby>岩<rt>いわ</rt></ruby>や <ruby>木<rt>き</rt></ruby>に なにかを <ruby>書<rt>か</rt></ruby>いては いけません。

Don't throw away your garbage; bring it home with you instead. Do not write anything on the mountain's rocks or trees.

<ruby>富士山<rt>ふじさん</rt></ruby>の トイレは、チップを <ruby>入<rt>い</rt></ruby>れる <ruby>箱<rt>はこ</rt></ruby>が あります。いつも きれいに する <ruby>人<rt>ひと</rt></ruby>のためです。100<ruby>円<rt>えん</rt></ruby>から 300<ruby>円<rt>えん</rt></ruby>くらいです。コインを <ruby>持<rt>も</rt></ruby>って <ruby>行<rt>い</rt></ruby>って ください。

The bathrooms on Mount Fuji have boxes where you can leave tips for the people who clean them. A typical tip is about ¥100 to ¥300, so be sure to bring a little change with you for that.

病気・医療
Illness and Medical Treatment

ある日、スリは、急に とても おなかが 痛くなりました。普通の 病気ではないかもしれない と思いましたが、どの病院に 行けば いいか わかりません。それで 近くの 病院に 行きました。

One day, Suri suddenly got a terrible stomachache. It didn't seem like a normal illness to her, but she didn't know which hospital to go to. So, she went to a nearby hospital.

"My stomach hurts...
 Which hospital??"

"There's a clinic nearby!"

(Kuma Orthopedics)

"Your stomach hurts?
Did you hit it on something? Or fall?"
(butsuke...?) "Um...yes...?" (It's a man!)

"Where is it?"
"I think I'm okay now..." (scary!)

病院を調べる
Looking for a hospital

日本語が よく わからなかったり、どの 病院に 行けば いいか わからないときは、英語や 他の 言語でも だいじょうぶな 病院を インターネットで 探すことが できます。

If you don't understand Japanese well or are unsure which hospital to go to, you can look online for hospitals that offer services in English or other foreign languages.

＊ https://www.jnto.go.jp/emergency/jpn/mi_guide.html

＊ http://jmip.jme.or.jp/search.php

もし、旅行中で インターネットが 使えないときは、観光案内や ホテルの人に「外国人のための 病院は ありますか？」と 聞いてください。また、女性の 医者のほうが いい場合は、「女性の 医者が いますか？」と、聞いてください。

If you are on vacation and don't have access to the Internet, ask a tourist information center or the staff at your hotel if there are any hospitals for foreigners (*Gaikokujin no tame no byouin wa arimasu ka?*). If you prefer a female doctor, ask if there is one available.

＊ https://matcha-jp.com/jp/5473

＊ https://www.yolo-japan.com/ja/medical/service

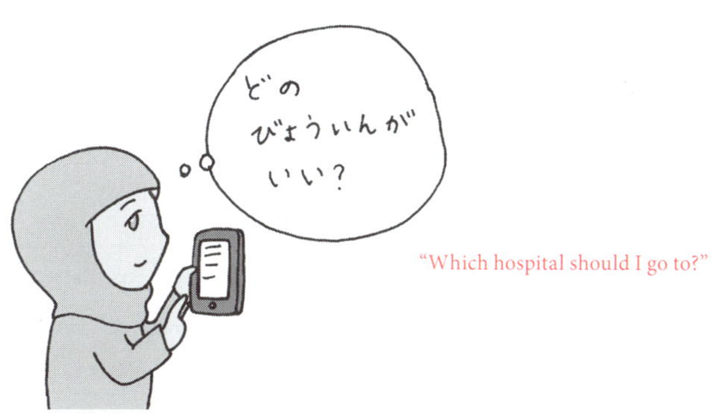

"Which hospital should I go to?"

病 院に行く　Going to a hospital or clinic

1. 受付　Reception

受付の人が「保険証と 診察券 ありますか？」と
聞きます。はじめてのときは、「はじめてです」と
言ってください。

The receptionist will ask you "Do you have an insurance card and a clinic card?" If it is your first time, say *hajimete desu* ("This is my first visit.").

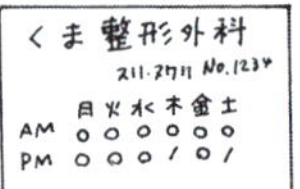

診察券：それぞれの 病 院の 時間や 患者の 番号が 書いてあります。病 院で 作ってくれます。

Clinic card: This lists your patient ID and the hospital hours. Each hospital or clinic will make one for you.

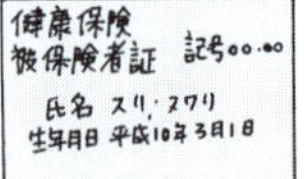

保険証：日本に 長く 住んでいる 人は 国か 会社の 保険を 使うことが できます。旅行の場合は、海外旅行保険を 使ったほうが いい です。日本に 来てから 入ることも できます。

Insurance card: Long-term residents of Japan can use their company or government insurance. When traveling, it's wise to enroll in some form of traveler's insurance. You can also enroll in this type of insurance after arriving in Japan.

＊ https://matcha-jp.com/jp/9871

＊ https://www.tokiomarine-nichido.co.jp/en/

在留カード、パスポート、クレジットカードと 現金も 持っていったほうが いいです。

You should bring your resident card, passport, credit card, and some cash.

保険が なくて、お金が 払えない場合は 大使館に 相談してください。

If you don't have insurance and cannot pay, contact your country's embassy for assistance.

2. 問診票を書く　Filling out medical questionnaires

名前、年齢、痛い ところや、病気について 書きます。病院に 行く前に 問診票を 作ることが できる サイトが あります。

Enter your name and age then describe your pain or illness. Some websites provide questionnaires that you can complete prior to going to the clinic.

＊https://www.yolo-japan.com/ja/medical/service

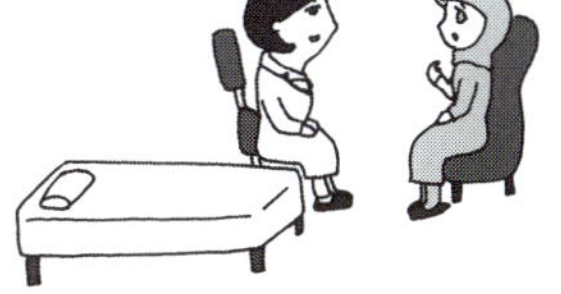

3. 診察　Medical exams and treatment

医者が 悪い ところを 検査したり、治療 したりします。

The doctor will examine your problem and provide treatment.

4. 会計　Payment

小さい 病院は 受付と 同じ ところで お金を はらいます。大きい 病院は、会計 という ところで お金を 払います。機械で 払う場合 も あります。

At small clinics, you can simply pay your bill at the reception desk. Large hospitals, however, have a designated place where payments are made. Sometimes, this is an automated machine.

5. 薬　Medication

たいてい、病院の ちかくに 薬局が あります。医者に もらった 紙 (処方せん) を 持って 行って、薬を もらいます。病院の中に 薬局が ある場合も あります。

Usually, there is a pharmacy near the clinic. Patients bring the paperwork (prescriptions) they get from their doctors then receive their medication. Some hospitals even have pharmacies inside them.

救急車の呼びかた　How to call an ambulance

救急車を 呼ぶためには、119に 電話を します。　To call an ambulance, dial 119.

火事ですか？ 救急ですか？
Is it a fire or medical emergency?

救急です。
A medical emergency.

場所は どこですか？
What is the location?

住所は ○○○○です。
The address is ○○○○.

＊住所が わからないときは、ちかくに ある 建物などを 言ってください。
　If you do not know the address, describe a nearby building or some other landmark.

どうしましたか？
What happened?

（症状を 言ってください）→ p.183-188
(Inform the operator of your symptoms.)

なまえ、ねんれい、電話番号を おしえてください。
Please tell me your name, age, and telephone number.

救急車が、あなたの 症状に 合った 病院に 連れて 行ってくれます。病気に よっては、遠い 病院に 行くことも あります。帰るときには 自分で タクシーなどで 帰らなければいけません。また、日本の 救急車は 無料で、たくさんの 人が 使うので、救急車が 足りないときが あります。軽い ケガ・病気のときなど、自分で 病院に 行けるときは、使わないほうが いいです。

The ambulance will take you to the hospital that is best equipped to handle your symptoms. This can be somewhat far away, depending on what's wrong with you. When returning home from the hospital, you'll have to find your own transportation (such as a taxi). Japanese ambulances are free, so many people use them unnecessarily and cause shortages for the patients who really need them. If your situation is not that serious and you can make it to the hospital on your own, you should refrain from calling an ambulance.

＊https://www.fdma.go.jp/publication/portal/post1.html

<ruby>巻末付録<rt>かんまつ ふ ろく</rt></ruby>

Appendix

点線で 本から 切り取って、病 院や レストランに 行くときに 使うこと
が できます。
お医者さんに 自分や 子どもの 症 状 を 伝えたり、店の人に 食べ物の
アレルギーや 制限を 伝えたりするときに 使ってください。

You can remove this appendix from the book and bring it with you to the
hospital, restaurant, etc.
Use it to convey your or your child's symptoms to a doctor or to inform
restaurant staff of your food allergies.

●p.181 ～ 188の使いかた

お医者さんに 自分や 子ども、家族の 症 状 を 伝えます。

1．p.181, 182のイラストを 使って、具合の よくないところを 指さして 伝えます。
2．p.183 ～ 188の表を 使って、症 状 を 指さして 伝えます。

How to use pages 181 through 188
Use the appendix to communicate the symptoms experienced by you, your child, or
another family member to a doctor.

1. You can point at the illustrations on pages 181 and 182 to indicate where the problem is
   on your body.

2. Then, use the information on pages 183 through 188 to inform the other party of your
   symptoms.

●p.189 ～ 191の使いかた

レストランや 食べ物を 売っている 店の人に、食べ物の アレルギーや 制限を 伝えます。

1．p.190の表から 食べられる・食べられない 食べ物を 選んで、p.189の（　　　）に 入
   れて 伝えます。
2．ヴィーガンや ムスリムの人は、p.191も 使って 食べ物の 制限を 伝えます。

How to use pages 189 through 191
These pages can help you inform the staff at restaurants and other places that sell food of
your food allergies and restrictions.

1. Select the items that you can and can't eat from the table on page 190, then enter them
   into the parentheses on page 189.

2. If you are vegan or Muslim, use page 191 to communicate your food restrictions.

体の部位 Parts of the body

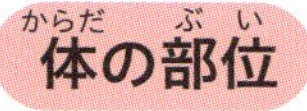

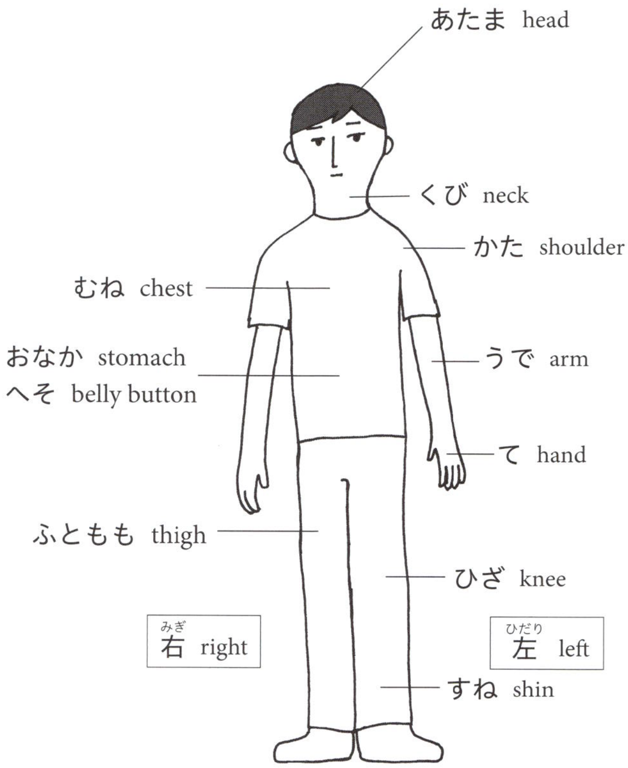

あたま head
くび neck
かた shoulder
むね chest
うで arm
おなか stomach
へそ belly button
て hand
ふともも thigh
ひざ knee
右 right
左 left
すね shin

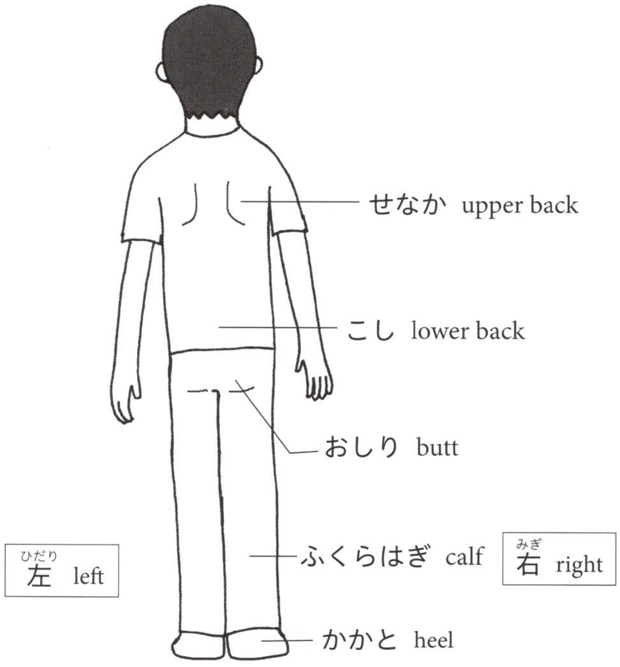

せなか upper back
こし lower back
おしり butt
左 left
ふくらはぎ calf
右 right
かかと heel

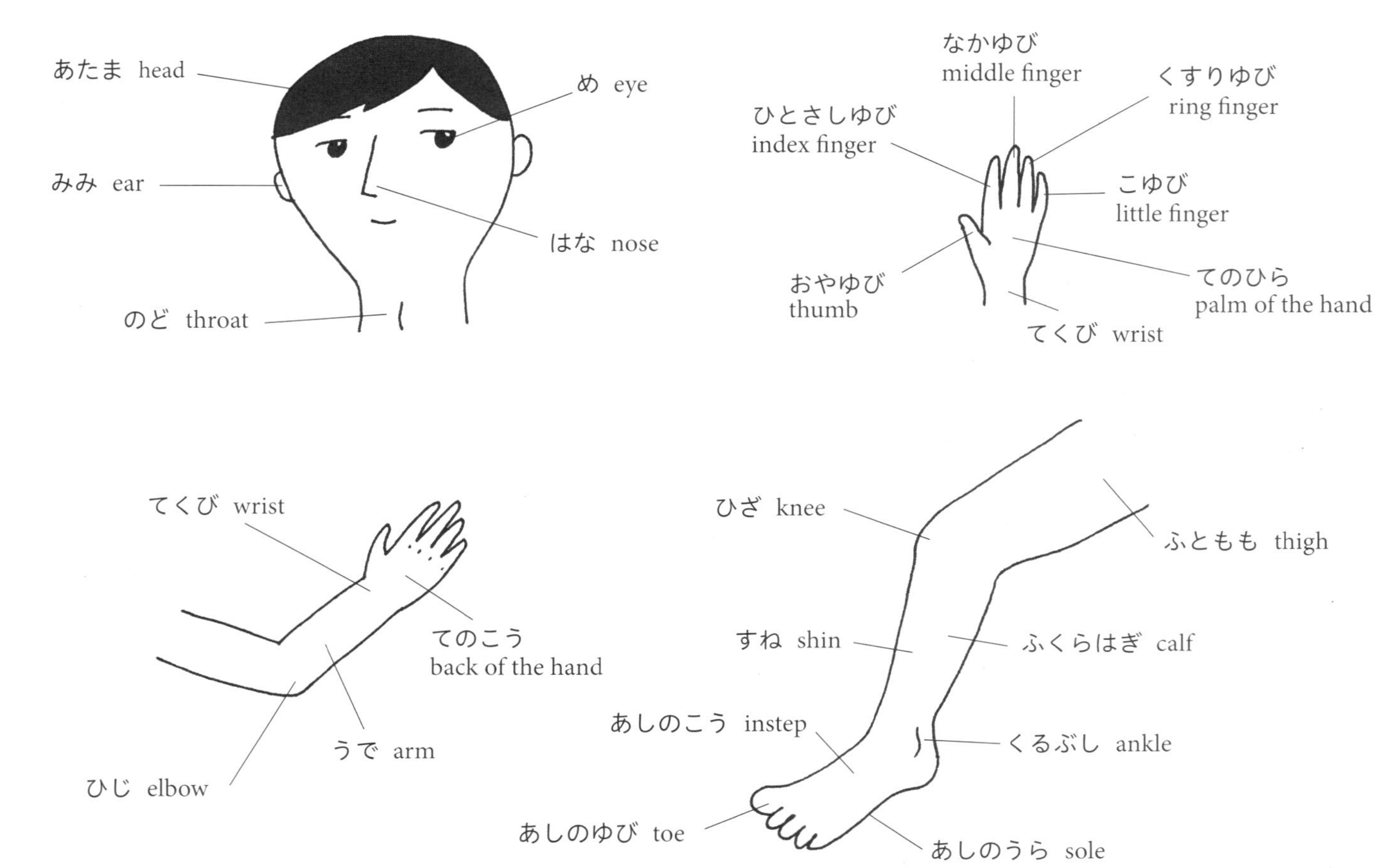

あたま head
め eye
みみ ear
はな nose
のど throat
なかゆび middle finger
くすりゆび ring finger
ひとさしゆび index finger
こゆび little finger
おやゆび thumb
てのひら palm of the hand
てくび wrist
てくび wrist
てのこう back of the hand
うで arm
ひじ elbow
ひざ knee
ふともも thigh
すね shin
ふくらはぎ calf
あしのこう instep
くるぶし ankle
あしのゆび toe
あしのうら sole

内科　Internal medicine

あたま いた 頭 が痛い headache	みぎ 右 right	ひだり 左 left	まえ 前 front	うし 後ろ back
	ずきずき throbbing	がんがん pounding	めまいがする feel dizzy	

ねつ 熱 fever	すこし slight	たかい high	だるい sluggish	き ぶん わる 気分が悪い Feel sick
	37 ℃ 98.6 °F	38 ℃ 100.4 °F	39 ℃ 102.2 °F	40 ℃ 104.0 °F

はなみず 鼻 水 runny nose	さらさら watery	ねばねば sticky		
	とうめい transparent	きいろ yellow		

せき 咳 cough	たくさん heavy	すこし light	たん 痰がでる to cough up phlegm
	いきぐる 息 苦しい difficulty breathing	ヒューヒュー wheezing (lightly)	ゼーゼー wheezing (heavily)

のど
throat

いたい	声が出ない	風邪
sore throat	to lose one's voice	(common) cold

胃
upper stomach

痛い	重い	吐く
hurts	heavy	vomit
きりきり	むかむか	
sharp pain	feel nauseous	

お腹
lower stomach

痛い	下痢	便秘	吐く
hurts	diarrhea	constipation	vomit

耳鼻科（じびか）　Ear, nose, and throat

耳（みみ）　ear

痛い（いた）　hurts

聞こえない（き）　can't hear

耳鳴り（みみな）　tinnitus

鼻（はな）　nose

鼻水（はなみず）　runny nose

鼻づまり（はな）　stuffy nose

さらさら　watery

ねばねば　sticky

とうめい　transparent

きいろ　yellow

眼科（がんか）　Ophthalmology

目（め）　eye

見えにくい（み）　can't see well

かゆい　itchy

違和感（いわかん）　discomfort

にょう
尿 / おしっこ
urine

はいにょうこんなん
排尿困難
difficulty urinating

けつにょう
血尿
blood in urine

はいにょうじ　いた
排尿時の痛み
pain when urinating

せいけい げ か
整形外科　Orthopedics

いた
痛い
hurts

しびれる
numb

ある
歩けない
can't walk

ま
曲げられない
can't bend

ケガ
injury

ころ
転んだ
fell

あたった
hit

こっせつ
骨折
broken bone

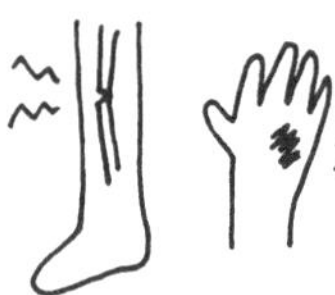

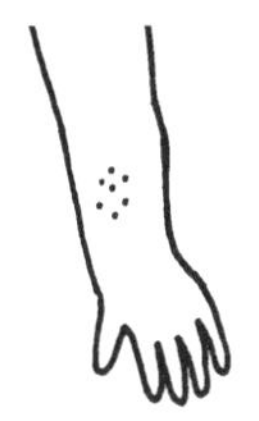

やけど burn	かゆい itchy	はっしん a rash
傷 injury	切る cut	すりむく skinned

歯科　Dental

歯が痛い toothache	しみる sensitive teeth	折れた broken

歯茎がいたい gum pain	歯のクリーニング teeth cleaning

せいり
生理
period

せいり　こ
生理が来ない
period is late

ふせいしゅっけつ
不正出血
irregular bleeding

にんしん
妊娠
pregnancy

にゅうぼう
乳房・おっぱい
breast

あか
赤ちゃん
baby

こ
子ども
child

な　つづ
泣き続けている
continuous crying

しょくじ
食事をしない
won't eat

げんき
元気がない
no energy

わたしは アレルギーが あります。

I have an allergy.

（　　　　　　　）を 食べる ことが できません。

I cannot eat （　　　　　）.

わたしは ベジタリアンです。

I am vegetarian.

（　　　　　　）は 食べません。

I cannot eat （　　　　　）.

（　　　　　　）は 食べる ことが できます。

I can eat （　　　　　）.

＊あなたの食べられる・食べられない食べ物を（　　）に入れてください。

Write the foods that you can and can't eat in the parentheses.

例 Examples

たまご	eggs	にゅう	milk	こむぎ	wheat
そば	buckwheat	大豆	soybeans	えび	shrimp
かに	crab	さば	mackerel	さけ	salmon
あわび	abalone	いか	squid	いくら	salmon roe
らっかせい	peanuts	アーモンド	almonds	カシューナッツ	cashews
くるみ	walnuts	まつたけ	matsutake mushrooms	やまいも	Japanese yams
トマト	tomatoes	セロリ	celery	玉ねぎ	onions
ニンジン	carrots	ホウレンソウ	spinach	オレンジ	orange
キウイフルーツ	kiwi	バナナ	bananas	もも	peaches
りんご	apples	いちご	strawberries	メロン	melon
牛肉	beef	豚肉	pork	鶏肉	chicken
ゼラチン	gelatin	グルテン	gluten		

わたしは ヴィーガンです。

I am vegan.

肉、魚、卵、乳製品、はちみつは 食べません。

I do not eat meat, fish, eggs, dairy products, or honey.

動物性の だしや、ソースも 食べることが できません。

I also cannot eat anything made from animal products,
such as soup stock or sauces.

わたしは ムスリムです。

I am Muslim.

豚肉は 食べません。

I do not eat pork.

豚骨や ラードの 入った 食品も とることが できません。

I also cannot eat foods that use bone broth
or lard made from pork.

やさ日まんが JAPAN ガイド

2022年 7月 4日 第1刷発行

著　者　小川　清美
発行者　浦　晋亮
発行所　IBCパブリッシング株式会社
〒162-0804 東京都新宿区中里町29番3号 菱秀神楽坂ビル
Tel. 03-3513-4511　Fax. 03-3513-4512
www.ibcpub.co.jp
印刷所　株式会社シナノパブリッシングプレス

ISBN978-4-7946-0719-5